THE HUMAN RIGHT TO LANGUAGE

THE HUMAN RIGHT TO LANGUAGE

Communication Access for Deaf Children

LAWRENCE M. SIEGEL

Gallaudet University Press
Washington, D.C.

Gallaudet University Press

Washington, DC 20002

http://gupress.gallaudet.edu

Library of Congress Cataloging-in-Publication Data

Siegel, Lawrence M., 1946–
The human right to language : communication access for deaf
children / Lawrence Siegel.
p. cm.
Includes bibliographical references and index.
ISBN-13: 978-1-56368-366-4 (alk. paper)
ISBN: 978-1-56368-591-0 (paperback)
1. Deaf—Legal status, laws, etc.—United States. 2. Hearing
impaired—Legal status, laws, etc.—United States. 3. Deaf
children—Education—United States. 4. Hearing impaired
children—Education—United States. 5. Deaf—Means of
communication. I. Title.
KF480.5.D4554   2008
344.73'079112—dc22   2008006662

This book is dedicated to my beloved daughter Elisabeth whose courage, determination, and big heart inspires me always.

CONTENTS

ACKNOWLEDGMENTS

I would like to thank Deirdre Mullervy and Karen Schoen for their steadfastness and professional skill in editing my writing, and Ivey Pittle Wallace for her support from the beginning, her patience with my impatience, and all-around ability, creativity, and insight.

I thank Gallaudet University for my appointment as the 2004–2005 Powrie V. Doctor Chair. My year at Gallaudet was a joyful experience and it provided me the time to research much of this book. I send my appreciation to Jay Innes and Joseph Fischgrund for their longstanding support of the work I have done and their help in developing the kind of language-driven educational paradigm that deaf and hard of hearing students deserve.

To my friend and colleague Ron Stern for whom my admiration has no limits.

As always, to my wife Gail.

This book is written in memory of my beloved daughter Catie. Her smile remains vivid and guides me.

PROLOGUE

Language is so tightly woven into human experience that it is scarcely possible to imagine life without it.

—Steven Pinker, *The Language Instinct*

FROM AFAR, certain moments in American history appear much starker than they may have been at the time. And yet in hindsight, we look back and are surprised by the previous lay of the land. We wonder how that could have been. As I consider the ways in which deaf and hard of hearing children have been denied that which is essential for educational growth, indeed any human growth at all—communication and language–I return to *Brown v. Board of Education*,[1] perhaps the most important legal case in American history. Before *Brown*, the previous rules and beliefs that governed a legally segregated nation had been in place for so long that their weight seemed immovable. In 1896, the Supreme Court ruled in *Plessy v. Ferguson* that an African American could be denied a seat on a train solely because of his race.[2] The *Plessy* decision made racial segregation the law of the land.

The rationales given for the maintenance of legal segregation, including states' rights, had been cited so often and with such emotional intensity and intellectual sleight of hand that one could not imagine anything different. Then came *Brown* and, in hindsight, we are or should be stunned by the previous status quo. How could that have been?

We know what followed, and still follows, but realize with shame that in the world's leading democracy, the law of the land at the time of the *Brown* case prevented a child from entering a public school solely because of his or her race. We are surprised or ashamed not because we are naive or do not know our history but because such a rule was so clearly contrary to our Declaration of Independence and our Constitution.

There is another moment to consider, one reflective of a system less deadly than slavery and Jim Crow but devastating nonetheless, full of profound consequences for the children I speak about. Whereas *Brown* represented a break from a historic failure, this other moment represented the formalization of a failure. As *Brown* moved children away from isolation, this other moment extended and legalized the isolation of many deaf and hard of hearing children.

In 1982, the U.S. Supreme Court ruled that Amy Rowley, a deaf child in a public school, was not entitled to have a sign language interpreter.[3] This meant, simply and directly, that she could not access a good deal of the language around her. Without the interpreter, the rich and varied language between teacher and student and between student and student was as far away for Amy as the "whites only" school across town was for the African American child in 1953. As of early 2008, the *Rowley* decision remains the law of the land and continues to be the deaf or hard of hearing child's *Plessy*. And so we ask, how can this be?

The American classroom is a marketplace of ideas in which our constitutional freedoms may be most vital. It also provides a unique environment in which a child is exposed to a varied and rich amalgam of social, intellectual, emotional, and academic discourse that floats around the child just as air surrounds all of us. The Supreme Court was content to allow Amy Rowley little of the air required to function and grow, and so deaf and hard of hearing children continue in the same suffocating world.

Amy Rowley has long since grown up, but she remains everybody's child, and we must view her isolation as we would view the isolation of our own children. It is difficult to compare the inequities of history, and although the inhumanities that *Brown* attempted to remedy were of a truly terrible stripe, the laws and policies visited upon Amy and other deaf and hard of hearing children over the years are harmful in their own fundamental way. A child who is unable to understand a lecture on *Brown*, who cannot communicate with a friend about plans for Friday night, and who lacks the language necessary to become a literate and functioning adult requires us to ask, again, how can that be?

The two teams of attorneys in the *Brown* case employed dozens of experts and submitted thousands and thousands of pages of legal arguments to the U.S. Supreme Court; oral argument was extensive. At the end of a particularly long day, James Madison Nabrit Jr., a young lawyer from Texas who had represented Indian tribal oil rights and fought off the Ku Klux Klan, stood before the Court and considered the technical discussion that had preceded him, but said, simply, that the issue here is about "liberty" and you "either have liberty or you do not" and that when liberty is "interfered with by the state" you cannot "justify it by saying that we only took a little liberty."[4]

Amy Rowley, without an interpreter, could understand about half of what was said in her classroom—provided the speaker sat very close to her, used only a few words, and spoke very slowly, and provided there was no significant surrounding noise. Perhaps the Court saw this as a "little liberty," for it judged it enough for Amy. Mr. Nabrit's notion resonates fully with the argument of this book, namely, that the denial of communication and language to children who are deaf or hard of hearing is liberty affecting, for when a deaf or hard of hearing child like Amy Rowley sits alone in a crowded classroom and is unable to access the rich and varied communication about her, she is denied any chance of success in life as surely as the plaintiffs in *Brown* were.

In this book I propose that the right to communication and language requires the protection of the U.S. Constitution. It is my contention that the First and Fourteenth Amendments to our Constitution mandate that Amy Rowley and other deaf and hard of hearing children have that which virtually every other American child takes for granted—the right to exchange ideas and information in school—and that current federal law violates those constitutional rights. Some may ask why this issue has not been raised before or whether the First Amendment, for example, already protects the rights I claim have no such protection. The short, and even surprising, answer here is that there are no judicial decisions or laws that recognize this "missing" right.

My express purpose in writing this book is to provide examples of the ways in which deaf and hard of hearing children are denied access to communication and language in school and to suggest a legal strategy to ensure their right to communication. Current policy, programs, and the underlying law, specifically the Individuals with Disabilities Education Act (IDEA), are in conflict with sound educational notions of growth, common sense, broad human rights, and constitutional principles. Whether the matter is taken up by those in the legal, educational, or Deaf communities remains to be seen. Whether or not the rationale offered in these pages is persuasive to our national and state legislatures or, if necessary, in our courts, I am convinced that significant efforts are required to change the status quo.

Ultimately, I am arguing that the rights recognized under both the First and Fourteenth Amendments must be enlarged to include a right broader than freedom of speech—a right to access and develop communication and language. For Amy and other deaf or hard of hearing children this means a right to communicate in school and to access programs that all other students access without any thought; it means providing the services and programs necessary to enforce these rights, whether through qualified interpreters, easy access to language-rich programs that are currently disfavored, or programs that provide language development. If all American students have the right to learn to read in order to engage in a full educational experience and become literate, then certainly there must be a right to learn and access language, the linchpin of all that follows, including literacy.

Charles Bradlaugh wrote in the nineteenth century that without the freedom to communicate, there can be "no discovery of truth." Better, he argued, a "thousandfold abuse" by those who communicate than a denial of the right, for the "abuse dies in a day, but the denial slays the life of the people."[5] The application of our Constitution to deaf and hard of hearing children will reflect well on who we are and on our unique institutions. To help a child express and receive ideas and information, complain about an intrusive classmate, exult over a small triumphant moment, delight in learning how to find the area of a triangle or what Monet was trying to convey through color, is to aid that child and enliven and reinvigorate our Constitution. And it will allow us to finally say about Amy Rowley, how could that have been?

NOTES

1. *Brown v. Board of Education*, 347 U.S. 483 (1954).
2. *Plessy v. Ferguson*, 163 U.S. 537 (1896).
3. *Board of Education v. Rowley*, 458 U.S. 176 (1982).
4. Richard Kruger, *Simple Justice* (New York: Vintage Books, 1975), 127, 583.
5. Edmund Fuller, *Thesaurus of Quotations* (New York: Crown, 1941), 398.

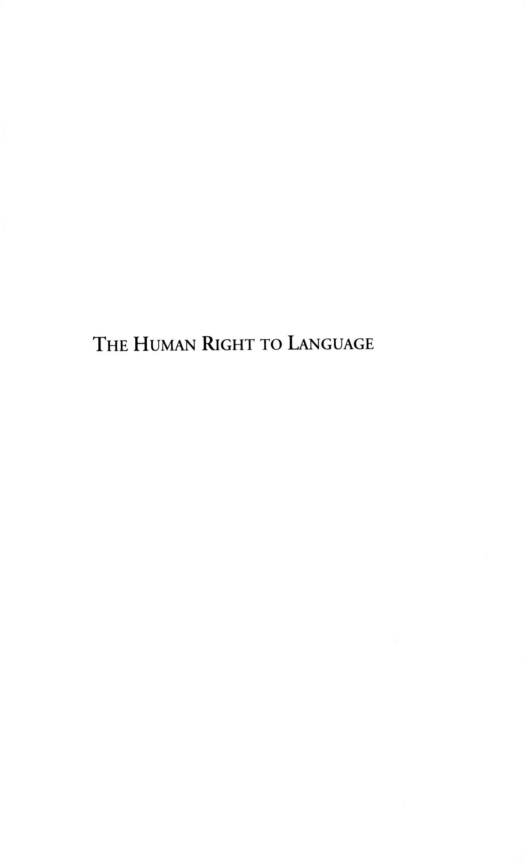

THE HUMAN RIGHT TO LANGUAGE

PART 1: COMMUNICATION AND LANGUAGE

1

INTRODUCTION

The limits of my language means the limits of my world.
—Ludwig Wittgenstein, *Tractatus Logico*

Amy Rowley was six when her parents asked her school to provide a sign language interpreter and the school declined their request. She was ten by the time the U.S. Supreme Court ruled that she had no right to the interpreter and therefore no right to access classroom communication and express her thoughts in school.* Amy Rowley's case has ever since represented, and will represent throughout this book, a stunning denial of the fundamental American right to access language and information and to be treated equally.

Amy had some residual hearing in the lower frequencies, which meant that she could distinguish vowels, and she had some speechreading (commonly known as lipreading) skills. Although most of us who can hear think that the ability to read lips allows one to understand what others are saying, the best lipreaders can detect no more than about 35 percent of what is visible on the lips. Consider the sentences you hear during the day. Remember that they are preceded and succeeded by other sentences of greater or lesser complexity in the ongoing flow of language; they may be spoken slowly or quickly, may be delivered in a clear or unclear manner, and may be affected by other sounds in the environment. Now take out half or three-quarters of what you hear. This was Amy's day in school.

Amy's parents were deaf, so Amy was exposed to sign language early in her life. She was unusual because 90 percent of deaf children

---

*Although I discuss at greater length in this book the complex issue of "interpreted" communication, it is important to note here that the real issue was not whether an interpreter would have provided truly effective language access for Amy (many argue with great force that interpreted education is at best a less isolating experience than no interpreter at all), but rather that communication and language access is so little valued for deaf and hard of hearing children.

have hearing parents.[1] She entered school with "a much better ability to communicate and receive information" than most deaf children. Amy had a high IQ, worked hard, and did well in kindergarten.[2]

Amy's education came under the federal special-education law, the Individuals with Disabilities Education Act (IDEA).* There are two fundamental failings under the IDEA that form the basis for this book's constitutional thesis: (1) the right to (and a recognition of the need for) language and communication *access* and *development* is not mandated and in many cases not only is of secondary importance but is in fact devalued under the IDEA; and (2) the placement requirement under the IDEA thwarts programmatic decisions that would encourage language and communication access and development. These two factors are discussed below and throughout this book.

The IDEA created important mandates for public schools and entitlements for children with disabilities, including the right to educational programs specifically tailored to meet their unique needs. There are three main requirements under the IDEA: (1) the provision of an individualized program, (2) with support services, (3) in the least restrictive environment (LRE).[3] A child's special needs, and the services required to meet them, are described in the child's individualized education program (IEP).

The LRE provision requires, absent very special circumstances, that children with disabilities be educated in a regular classroom. However, this placement can be highly isolating, and therefore more restrictive, for many deaf children. A deaf child who uses sign language and is placed in a regular classroom will often have few, if any, peers or staff members with whom he or she can directly communicate (and without, for example, an interpreter, communication ends). Placement in a legally more "restrictive" environment—a center or state school where there is a critical mass of language peers—will provide a truly linguistically inclusive education. One consequence of the LRE mandate is to increase rather than decrease isolation for many deaf and hard of hear-

*The IDEA (codified at 20 U.S.C. §§ 1400 *et seq.*) was enacted in 1975 as the Education for All Handicapped Children Act (Pub. L. No. 94-142, 89 Stat. 773). It has been reauthorized numerous times by the U.S. Congress, most recently in 2004.

ing children, an irony in light of *Brown v. Board of Education*.* The LRE requirement adds to the complexity of the issues facing deaf and hard of hearing children and results in the devaluing of their communication and language needs. The burden on the deaf child to prove that he or she needs and is entitled to a rich language program is severe: the IDEA states that a child cannot be "removed" from a regular classroom unless there is proof that the child cannot "achieve satisfactorily" even with the use of supplementary aids and services.[4] The deaf child must fail before that child can access a school environment in which he or she can communicate with peers and teachers. This is hardly an outcome or process that suggests a "least restrictive environment" for many deaf children.

The IDEA provides that when the school and family disagree about some aspect of the child's program, either may request a due process hearing in which a neutral third party takes evidence and issues a decision. This decision can be appealed all the way to the U.S. Supreme Court.

At the Rowley due process hearing, the school district introduced evidence that Amy was doing well academically and therefore did not need an interpreter. It also submitted evidence that without the interpreter Amy could still access about 60 percent of classroom communication. There are significant questions, however, about the accuracy of this figure, The evaluation took place in a quiet area. Amy sat with an evaluator who spoke one word at a time; Amy then tried to identify the spoken word by pointing to one of four pictures. In this setting she was able to identify 60 percent of the spoken information. That this environment did not equate to the lively and noisy classroom is evident. The difference between a one-word expression in a test setting and the greater complexity of classroom communication is profound. Accordingly, it is likely that Amy missed a good deal more than 40 percent of classroom communication. Perhaps the best way to consider the half-empty–half-full nature of this 60/40 percent figure is to ask any parent how he or she would feel if his or her child was denied 40 percent of what is communicated in school.

*I would argue that the IDEA and our educational system are capable of understanding the subtle but important differences between children and that racial segregation is in many ways like the linguistic segregation that many deaf children experience.

The fair-hearing officer ruled in favor of the school district; no interpreter was required. At that point, Amy's family had only one option to secure full language access for Amy—go to court. Although initially this option represents a considerable "extra" right (after all, parents of non-special-education children usually cannot go to court over a programmatic issue), it is a mixed blessing. What parent wants to have to go to court to secure such fundamental educational rights? What parent wants to go to a meeting to convince the school that such access is justified, and then if unsuccessful, fight through administrative hearings and courts to secure his or her child's right to know what is going on in the classroom? And, perhaps, do this every year of the child's educational life?

Amy's parents appealed the administrative decision to a federal district court, which found that even though Amy was in the relatively simple communication environment of kindergarten and interacted "fairly well" with her classmates, her opportunities to interact were no more than "superficial." The court concluded that Amy had a bright future and should have the chance to "achieve her full potential commensurate with the opportunity provided to other children." The judge recognized that the issue was not that hearing children actually access 100 percent of the communication in their environment but that they have 100 percent access if they want it. An interpreter would give Amy nearly that same opportunity. The federal district court judge reversed the hearing officer's decision and ordered the school district to provide Amy Rowley with a sign language interpreter.[5]

The school district appealed the district court's ruling, and the federal appellate court affirmed the decision requiring the provision of the sign language interpreter for Amy.[6] The school district then appealed to the U.S. Supreme Court. It was the first IDEA case to reach the country's highest court. The Supreme Court ruled that

- Amy was a very "well-adjusted" child;
- she was receiving an "adequate" education;
- the IDEA did not promise that a child would meet his or her full potential;
- courts should not substitute their judgment for a school's decision; and
- if a child is progressing from grade to grade, regardless of how much communication access he or she may or may not have, the law requires no more.[7]

IT IS PERPLEXING that the Supreme Court focused on whether the law required that Amy's potential be maximized rather than on the quite different and more fundamental issues of Amy's right to the free flow of information in her classroom (under the First Amendment) and her right to be treated the same as any other student, including the right to have access to surrounding communication (under the Fourteenth Amendment). To understand Amy's isolation at its most basic level, one merely needs to think of his or her own child in a classroom, day after day, year after year, able to access little of what the teacher and other children are discussing. The Supreme Court's decision, which amounts to the deaf child's *Plessy v. Ferguson*—perhaps without the venality but with real and painful consequences—remains the law of the land. Every deaf and hard of hearing child in this nation is subject to its reach and meaning. Every deaf and hard of hearing child who steps into a public school in this nation is subject to *Rowley* and its narrow view of the importance of communication and language.*

*When the IDEA was reauthorized in 1997 by the U.S. Congress, new language was added requiring that the IEP team (family and school personnel) discuss a deaf or hard of hearing child's "communication needs." Although this was a welcome change, it did not and still does not create any requirement to provide the access Amy was denied. Deaf and hard of hearing children still have no right to language access but merely the right to debate its merit in the IEP. Discussing an educational need and being required to provide it are two very different things.

The IDEA includes a list of specific related services that a child may need in order to benefit from his or her education. In 2004, the U.S. Congress added a sign language interpreter to this list. The IDEA does not, however, mandate that any of the listed related services be provided to a student. The decision, like any other part of the child's education and IEP, is one that must be made by the parents and the school district; the latter is not required to provide a related service if it does not believe the child needs it.

Since the passage of the IDEA in 1975 and Amy Rowley's appearance before the U.S. Supreme Court in 1982, thousands of IEPs have been written, hundreds of due process hearings have been held, and dozens of court decisions involving deaf children have been issued. The stories of these children tell us a good deal about the central value and necessity of communication and language, as well as how our educational system and the law of the land fail to provide for them.

By a *right to communication and language*, I mean broadly the right to *access* and *develop* language, I mean, more specifically,

1. the broad process of receiving and expressing information and ideas, the very access denied to Amy Rowley;
2. the right to communicate easily and directly with classmates and with teachers;
3. unfettered access to programs with a critical mass of age and language peers, even though these programs are disfavored under the IDEA;*
4. the provision of services and programs that facilitate communication and language access and development;
5. the presence of qualified teachers, interpreters, note takers, and other professionals to assist the child's easy and daily access to his or her language;
6. the right to one's communication mode, whether oral-aural or visual;
7. the right to one's language, whether English, American Sign Language (ASL), or signing systems for those children who use them;
8. the presence of staff who can communicate directly and

*Day schools and state residential schools for the deaf have historically provided deaf and hard of hearing children what local schools and programs cannot: a mass of peers who use the same communication mode and language. The IDEA's LRE requirement has created a significant barrier to such programs, as evidenced by the closing of state schools since the passage of the IDEA in 1975.

proficiently in a signing child's native language and communication mode;

9. the availability of support services and acoustically treated classrooms for deaf and hard of hearing children who express and receive communication orally, to ensure their meaningful participation in education;

10. the hiring of staff who are fully trained in working with deaf and hard of hearing students who have residual hearing and use their aural and oral skills for receiving and expressing language; and

11. the unquestioned right to access and develop language, just as there is no question that all hearing children can access language in their schools and develop the ability to read, write, and compute.

None of these are required or even mentioned under the IDEA.

Although deaf and hard of hearing children are highly capable of functioning in the hearing world—they "are capable of the same cognitive development" as their hearing peers—the differences between the children in this group are significant.[8] They may communicate through sign language or be exclusively oral in their communication mode. They may have hearing aids or cochlear implants. They may have learning disabilities or other complications, or they may be Phi Beta Kappa candidates. They may need a sign language interpreter or an acoustically treated classroom to ensure that they can maximize their residual hearing. They may be part of a well-defined culture and community—the Deaf community—or have little or no connection with the Deaf world.* The

*It may seem that a deaf person who has good oral skills and who has grown up and been educated in the hearing world will function, to a greater or lesser degree, effectively in that world. It is more complex than that. Many, particularly those who are hard of hearing, feel rooted in neither the deaf nor the hearing worlds. They have no exposure to ASL, the language of the Deaf community, and have not been educated with other deaf people, but at the same time they function only on the margins of

linguistic needs of a deaf child like Amy Rowley are fundamentally different from those of a child who lost his hearing at ten, has well-developed English skills, and retains some hearing. This child is really much closer experientially and linguistically to a hearing child than to Amy.

There is an ongoing and heated debate over oral versus manual language, ASL versus English-based signing systems. It is my position that all deaf and hard of hearing children should have the right to access and develop communication and language in a way that meets their unique linguistic needs. The debate over which way is "right" or "best" is an argument lost before it begins. To argue that the school system should provide only oral-aural options, only signing systems, or only ASL is to ignore the subtle and important differences between these children and to deny them what is their right. It also, in a sad and perhaps unintentional way, allows policymakers and educators to avoid the difficult issues before them about language development and communication access. This book is about law and societal values, not about limiting linguistic options; to focus on the latter only diminishes the former.

Because the IDEA is the law of the land regarding special education, and because the U.S. Supreme Court has confirmed the underlying and limited use of the IDEA for many deaf and hard of hearing children, it is my belief that no real significant change in the education of deaf and hard of hearing children will occur until there is a clearly recognized legal, constitutional right to communication and language. As currently written, the IDEA is fundamentally out of tune with the communication and language needs of deaf and hard of hearing children and, frankly, violates their First and Fourteenth Amendment rights.*

the hearing world. Many, but not all, eventually end up moving toward and into the Deaf community, where a new world opens up for them. *See* Gina A. Oliva, *Alone in the Mainstream* (Washington, D.C.: Gallaudet University Press, 2001).

*Over the years, concerted efforts have been made to rewrite the IDEA to include the unique language needs of deaf and hard of hearing children. Those efforts have failed to significantly change the IDEA for

The need to communicate in school simply cannot be reduced to a disputed IEP agenda item. It is too precious and necessary a need to be subject to debate. Parents are not required to prove to their child's teachers and school administrators that a reading program is necessary; nor do they need to convince teachers and administrators (or a hearing officer or judge) of this every year of the child's school life. Parents of deaf and hard of hearing children should not have to prove the need for communication access and development. They would gladly give up their rights to go to IEP meetings and hearings and courts to secure that which is taken for granted by every other child in this nation.

The vignettes that begin each chapter in this book speak directly to the failure of public-school programs to provide communication and language for deaf and hard of hearing children. Many of the vignettes are taken directly from reported cases. Others are taken, either in whole or in part, from my experiences or experiences reported to me by parents and colleagues. Some represent a composite of those stories. All the vignettes represent real and often-repeated experiences of deaf and hard of hearing children in this nation.

The right to communication, the need to envelope a deaf child within the Constitution, is fundamentally right and fair, and is reflected in both these stories and the legal analysis that follows. We should look to those fundamental American rights to exchange ideas and information, as embodied in the First Amendment, and to be treated equally, as reflected in the Fourteenth Amendment, and apply them to deaf and hard of hearing children. Our Constitution is flexible and grand enough to embrace them.

two reasons: (1) a lack of real understanding of the unique communication and language needs of deaf and hard of hearing children and (2) the fact that legislators are not likely to make changes that will add what they think will be significant costs to the system. Legislative change (without litigation) is unlikely.

In 1816, Thomas Jefferson wrote about constitutional flexibility, his words inscribed on the wall of the Jefferson Memorial.

> Laws and institutions must go hand in hand with the progress of the human mind. As that becomes more developed, more enlightened, as new discoveries are made, new truths discovered and manners and opinions change, with the change of circumstances, institutions must advance also to keep pace with the times. We might as well require a man to wear still the coat which fitted him when a boy as civilized society to remain ever under the regimen of their barbarous ancestors.[9]

Deaf and hard of hearing children should no longer be made to wear the ill-fitting coat of another time.

Notes

1. For a discussion of the often-overwhelming experience for hearing parents and, of course, the deaf child, there are a number of excellent books, including the early *They Grow in Silence*, by Eugene D. Mindel and McCay Vernon (Silver Spring, Md.: National Association of the Deaf, 1971). Hearing parents often go through difficult stages—grief, anger, denial—and, of equal importance, are too infrequently provided a full range of information on options available to them and their children. They want their child to be "normal," and thus in those cases in which the child is profoundly and prelingually deaf (i.e., loses hearing before language is developed), the failure to expose the child to early sign language can be devastating. See also "The Development of Deaf and Hard of Hearing Children Identified Early through the High-Risk Registry," by Christine Yoshinaga-Itano and Mah-Rya L. Apuzzo, *American Annals of the Deaf,* 143 (1998): 416, 423, in which the authors assess the obvious but nonetheless highly important view that the earlier language is provided to a deaf (or any) child, the better will be the chance of normal language and therefore cognitive development.

2. *Rowley v. Board of Education,* 483 F. Supp. 528, 530 (S.D.N.Y. 1980).

3. The LRE requirement is found at 20 U.S.C. § 1412(a)(5). See *Board of Education v. Holland*, 786 F. Supp. 874 (E.D. Cal. 1992), and *Campbell v. Talladega*, 518 F. Supp. 47 (N.D. Ala. 1981), for a discussion of Congress's focus on mainstreaming as a central part of the IDEA.

4. 20 U.S.C. § 1412(a)(5).

5. *Rowley*, 483 F. Supp. 528.

6. *Rowley v. Board of Education*, 632 F.2d 945 (2d Cir. 1980).

7. *Board of Education v. Rowley*, 458 U.S. 176 (1982).

8. Brenda Schick, "How Might Learning through an Educational Interpreter Influence Cognitive Development?" in *Educational Interpreting: How It Can Succeed*, ed. Elizabeth A. Winston (Washington, D.C.: Gallaudet University Press, 2004), 74.

9. Letter to Samuel Kercheval, July 12, 1816, as inscribed on the Jefferson Memorial, Washington, D.C.

2

THE IMPORTANCE
OF COMMUNICATION
AND LANGUAGE

Language is not only the vehicle of thought, it is a great and efficient instrument in thinking.

—Sir Humphry Davy

Carol was a bright, lively young girl with an easy-going personality and a keen interest in horses. She did well in school and enjoyed literature and math. Others saw her as calm and strong, so much so that they were unaware of her isolation. She had some residual hearing, and if she was in a quiet room and one person spoke clearly and slowly, she could discriminate some of what was being said. If that dynamic shifted even a bit, if the speaker turned away, if noise came from somewhere else in the room, if another sixteen-year-old dropped a book or asked the teacher a question—in short if there was more than one clear, distinguishable, and direct expression of language—Carol was lost.

When she was younger and language was at a relatively simple level—one- and two-word expressions, language of limited vocabulary—Carol's classmates would try to communicate with her. They would slowly mouth "hello" or "Do you want to go outside at recess?" but children will not long tolerate a lag in response. One of Carol's early teachers taught the class rudimentary signs—HELLO, HOW ARE YOU? WHAT IS YOUR NAME?—and for a while the students used these signs, but it was a superficial, stagnant mode of communicating, and the signs were soon forgotten.

By the third or fourth grade, at a time when socialization becomes more complex, Carol began to feel more isolated from her classmates. It was not that they were unkind; they just tended to ignore her. Her exchanges with other students went from occasional to infrequent to rare. She did her homework during lunch and recess. She played soccer, but was never invited to anyone's house after school, on the weekends, or in the summer. No one consciously chose to exclude her; she just did not really exist. In return, she did not bother anyone; she simply stayed out of reach.

Carol had an interpreter for her academic high school classes, including English. The interpreter tried, but he was paid by the hour, he was not certified, and his vocabulary was incomplete, which meant that he often relied on fingerspelling.* He did his best but was always behind. He had two different responsibilities: (1) to convert spoken language into sign language for Carol and (2) to convert Carol's sign language into spoken language for the class.

One day, the teacher began the class by saying, "Some people think that Shakespeare and Freud had a lot in common. What do you think?"†

There was silence in the class while most of the students waited for someone else to take a chance. The teacher was a favorite at the school; though she was sometimes impatient, she loved the work, the students, and the subject matter. She had not objected to Carol's being placed in the class with a sign language interpreter.

Carol's interpreter signed the question as, "William Shakespeare. Freud. The same?"

A student raised her hand and said, "Well, I think because Shakespeare wrote about so many psychological things that maybe that is why they say he is kind of like Freud."

The interpreter then fingerspelled and signed the student's response, "S-h-a-k-e-s-p-e-a-r-e and p-s-y-c-h-o-l-o-g-i-c-a-l. He wrote about that—"

Before he got to the end of the student's response, the teacher was

---

*In ASL, the English alphabet is represented by handshapes for all the letters, *A* to *Z*. For example, the word *America* has a sign, but it can also be fingerspelled letter by letter: A-m-e-r-i-c-a. Unqualified interpreters sometimes leave out actual words and phrases, and they may misspell words (e.g., Shakespear). Thus the amount of information denied to deaf and hard of hearing students can be substantial.

†It is vital that the reader take the time to experience the entire classroom exchange. It is not easy to read the simultaneous discussions, just as it clearly was not easy for Carol to follow them in class. Numerous deaf colleagues and friends have indicated that the vignette is a powerful and realistic example of the isolation they feel.

already asking another question. "What plays do you think are psychological thrillers, so to speak?"

A second student answered, "Well, *Macbeth* for sure and *Hamlet.*"

Carol's interpreter stopped interpreting the comment by the first student, began to sign the teacher's question, "p-s-y-c-h-o-l-o-g-i-c-a-l t-h-r-i-l-l-e-r-s," but stopped to try to capture the second student's response to the teacher, "M-a-c-b-e-t-h sure—"

Teacher: "Okay, but the rest of the class, what is it about these plays that—"

Interpreter: "and H-a-m-l—"

Second Student: "In *Macbeth* there is all that guilt—"

Teacher (smiling): "You mean, 'Out, out damn spot?' What do you make of that, Dr. Freud?"

Interpreter: "In those plays, what do you mean 'out d-a-m-n spot. Dr. F-r-e—"

Third Student: "The mind is playing a trick, trying to wash out the guilt for the crime."

Teacher: "And what about *Hamlet?* What is your diagnosis there?"

Interpreter: "—g-u-i-l-t—"

Fourth Student: "All that mother and son stuff and Oedipal deals—"

Interpreter: "—d-i-a-g-n-o-s-i-s—"

Teacher: "This is pretty universal and ancient stuff; what about Oedipus Rex, Sigmund, and William?"

Interpreter: "Old ideas about mothers and sons—O-d-a-p-u-s-s—S-i-g—W-l-l-i-a-m?"

Teacher: "The ancients, you see, understood the unconscious, even if they didn't give it a name or fully comprehend its impact on us as Sigmund Freud understood. Guilt and hatred and those things go to the root of our being, and Shakespeare, as a genius of language and psychology, understood this."

Interpreter: "U-n-c-o-n-s-c-i-o-u-s at the root that S-h-a-k—"

Fifth Student: "Was Shakespeare neurotic?"

Interpreter: "language and p-s-y-c-h-o-l-o-g-y—N-e-u-r-o-t-i-c—understood this."

Teacher: "Funny man, Carl. You know Freud said that there was no such thing as just a joke, that it hid some unconscious things. Maybe we'll begin your analysis right here."

The class laughed at both Carl and the teacher, which gave Carol a chance to raise her hand. She signed rapidly, "I don't understand, neurotic and unconscious, what were you saying about *Hamlet?*" Carol's interpreter's receptive skills—his ability to read signs—were not very good; he voiced to the teacher and class, "I don't understand, neurology and conscience. What did Hamlet say?"

The teacher paused and asked the interpreter to repeat what he said. With five minutes left in the class, the teacher told Carol to carefully reread the scene where Hamlet's mother, Gertrude, dies. She then addressed the whole class. "So we see that Freud and the ancient Greeks and William Shakespeare share a good deal about the human psyche, and from them we learn much about ourselves. Just ask Carl. For tomorrow I'd like you to write a two-page essay on *Hamlet, Macbeth*, and Freud. See you tomorrow."

As the students rushed out to their next class, the interpreter was signing to Carol, "G-e-r-t-r-u-d-e—Finish tomorrow H-a-m-l-e M-a-c-b-e-t-h F-r—"

COMMUNICATION AND LANGUAGE AND THE HUMAN EXPERIENCE

COMMUNICATION AND LANGUAGE are central to the human experience, and the ability and need to convey thoughts, feeling, hopes, and information defines the human species. It is as profound and simple as that. From Aristotle to Benedict de (Baruch) Spinoza to Dylan Thomas to Andy Warhol, philosophers and artists have understood that communication and language make our world intelligible and available to us.

A society exists whenever the members of a group can convey ideas to one another. Some call this "deliberate communication," and its purpose is no less significant than to ensure that human beings are unified into one life and that the "development of the community as a continuous process of intercommunication and organization of experience" may proceed. Indeed, the "hypothesis of other minds would be untenable without the prior possibility of interpersonal communication."[1] Josiah Royce, a late-nineteenth-century philosopher, concluded that "without language . . . there would be no self."[2]

Suppose we had no word for a strawberry or nausea or coffee or a tear or capitalism; no language to express gravitation or death;

no way to communicate our understanding of, or confusion about, the relativity of time or why something makes us laugh. No way to convey, even partially, the feeling of love. Language is

> not just some superficial part of human thinking. We are not just apes who have dabbled with some special communication trick. Language is totally integrated into every aspect of human mental functioning. We are linguistic savants, lightning calculators of semantic and syntactic arithmetic. . . . This rare and anomalous cognitive ability is thus one of the most robust and irrepressible characteristics of our species.[3]

We start, then, with this notion of the beauty, uniqueness, authority, and necessity of communication and language. We know without any proof that we must communicate and convey thoughts through language, or we cease to be human. And this is true for those with or without hearing, for those who rely on oral-aural language as much as for those who rely on visual language.

THE DIFFERENCE BETWEEN COMMUNICATION AND LANGUAGE

There are important differences between the concepts of communication and language. *Communication* refers to the general way in which humans convey thoughts, feelings, and ideas to one another. Communication can take the form of a smile, a punch to the nose, a written note, the celebratory dance of a football player, and tens of thousands of other conveyances. *Communication* is defined as "a process by which information is exchanged between individuals through a common system of symbols, signs, or behavior." *Language* is defined as "a systematic means of communicating ideas or feelings by the use of conventionalized signs, sounds, gestures, or marks having understood meaning."[4]

Humans communicate and employ language. Deaf and hard of hearing individuals communicate in as many varied ways as hearing individuals. They communicate through written, oral-aural, and manual modes. They employ language as hearing individuals do, whether it be English or ASL.

If communication and language are central to our being, then it follows that our institutions, our laws, our Constitution, must recognize those values as well. Our democracy insists on our freedom, and our freedom depends on the free flow of information, on the exchange of thoughts through language. The need to access information, to have our say, to appreciate what others think and communicate, is central to our democracy and to our growth as individuals.

International law recognizes the importance of language and the right to it. Article 27 of the United Nations International Covenant on Civil and Political Rights provides that linguistic minorities shall not be denied the right to communicate with members of their community. This right creates an obligation to protect the identity and to ensure the survival and continuous development of linguistic minorities.[5]

The Universal Declaration of Linguistic Rights acknowledges the right to be part of, and to be recognized as a member of, a language community; the right to use one's own language both in private and public; the right for one's language and culture to be taught (Article 3); the right to acquire knowledge of one's own language (Article 13); and the right to an education that will enable the members of a language community to gain full command of their own language (Article 26). The declaration also recognizes that the rights of *all* language communities are equal (Article 5).[6] The United Nations Declaration on the Rights of Persons belonging to National or Ethnic, Religious, or Linguistic Minorities calls for states to provide opportunities to "receive instruction in their mother tongues."[7] Finally, the Hague Recommendations regarding the Education Rights of National Minorities suggest that education should be provided in a child's language and that a minority language should be taught as a subject on a regular basis.[8]

These conventions recognize that there is a significant connection between language and human dignity, that these rights must be protected not by other individuals but by governments, and that it is not "enough if the state only assumes an obligation not to interfere with" the linguistic development of children—the state in fact has a duty to enhance the right itself.[9] Many countries have taken steps and assumed these duties. South Africa recognizes sign language as an official language in school, and Uganda includes sign language in its constitution. Denmark and Sweden have long provided extensive sign language school programs.[10] Our government should have a similar duty, so that deaf and hard of hearing children do not continue to be subject to laws and policies that, consciously or otherwise, interfere with rather than support their language rights. Our Constitution cannot continue to be merely neutral; it must affirmatively protect this right.

DEAFNESS AND COMMUNICATION AND LANGUAGE

Hearing loss and its linguistic implications are profound. Many, if not most, hearing people assume that greater amplification will resolve a hearing problem. They have little understanding or even awareness that though some deaf people develop oral-aural skills, many use a viable and formal visual language that conveys thought as fully and effectively as spoken language.

Most hearing people cannot imagine living without sound. Yet many deaf people have told me that they would not become hearing even if they could, because their language, culture, and community are rich in things that hearing people don't have. It is a worthy point to be respected and understood and to consider within the context of the importance of, and the right to, communication and language.

Deaf and hard of hearing children are fully capable of developing and using language and of communicating. However, their needs for special accommodations to access language and communication, in whatever mode or language they use, are different from those of almost every other so-called disability group that the law and educational policy and programs address. All other children with disabilities, whether they are blind, use wheelchairs, or are developmentally delayed, can hear the teacher and their classmates. They know what is being said in the classroom just by being present. Deaf and hard of hearing children do not.

The issue of providing communication and language is made even more complex by the significant differences that exist between deaf and hard of hearing people. Approximately 13 million Americans have some measurable hearing loss, and 6.5 million have a bilateral loss (a loss in both ears). Demographers estimate that almost 500,000 Americans use ASL as their primary language and make up the Deaf community. That total is interesting in light of the number of people who speak other languages in the United States—approximately 400,000 speak French, 250,000 speak German, and 125,000 speak Yiddish.[11]

Individuals who lose their hearing at or just after birth are called *prelingually deaf,* and those who lose their hearing after developing language (usually after the age of two) are called *postlingually deaf.* Some prelingually deaf individuals rely exclusively on oral-aural language and have no signing skills at all. Other prelingually deaf people use only manual means of communicating. Some of these people use ASL, whereas others use signing systems developed to teach English to deaf children (e.g., Signed English and Signing Exact English). Still others communicate both orally and manually using English-based systems like Total Communication and Cued Speech.*

*Signing systems, which are generally intended to be visual representations of English, are profoundly different from ASL. A sentence conveyed through an English signing system would in fact look very much like standard written English. Every English word would have a singular corresponding sign. For example, the sentence "Today I will run from my home to the park" would have a sign for each of those words and the order would the same as in spoken English. Using ASL, the signer would es-

The number of people that use manual language (whether ASL or a signing system) or oral-aural language is hard to pinpoint. A survey during the 2002–2003 school year found that, of approximately 40,000 deaf and hard of hearing students, 18,237 (45 percent) were taught orally, 16,995 (42 percent) with speech and sign, and 3,753 (3 percent) with sign only.[12] The Gallaudet Research Institute found in 1995 that, of 43,861 deaf and hard of hearing children, 41 percent were exclusively oral, 56 percent used some combination of speech and sign, and 1.9 percent used ASL; in 2000, 44 percent were exclusively oral, 49 percent used a combination of speech and sign, and 5.8 percent used ASL.[13] During the 1999–2000 school year, less than 15 percent of students six to eleven years of age had cochlear implants; by the 2002–2003 school year, the figure was up to 22 percent, a significant increase with major implications for the future education of deaf and hard of hearing students.[14]

Educators, parents of deaf children, and Deaf adults have long argued over the best way to teach language to deaf children. Some say that exposure to and development of ASL is a prerequisite for the development of English skills and literacy, whereas others counter that literacy is best developed if deaf and hard of hearing children learn English orally or through an English-based signing system. Research increasingly shows that deaf children who develop a natural, manual language learn to read (and write) much like hearing children for whom English is a second language and that the development of a strong native linguistic base (whether oral or manual) is necessary for literacy growth.[15]

This communication debate has been raging for hundreds of years, with no end in sight. I make no attempt to suggest that one way is better than another. Ultimately, it is essential that parents understand the difference between a natural and formal language

tablish the place of the home and the park in the space in front of the body and would sign ME RUNNING while moving the hands from one place to the other.

and signing systems, as well as the difference between all manual options and oral-aural language. All families should be fully informed and knowledgeable so that the best decisions can be made for the deaf or hard of hearing child. Regardless of the parents' language-communication choice, all deaf and hard of hearing children should have access to what all other children in our nation take for granted—language and communication, the chance to develop English skills, and a rich educational environment in which they can communicate directly with their peers and teachers.

The need for communication and language illustrates the complex ways in which hearing loss is fundamentally different from any other disability. It underscores both the difficulties perpetuated by current law and policy and why communication and language access and development must become a right rather than an afterthought in our educational system. John Dewey said that "society exists in and through communication."[16] So it is for deaf and hard of hearing people.

NOTES

1. Elizabeth Flower and Murray G. Murphey, *A History of Philosophy in America* (New York: Putnam, 1977), 2:728–729, 751, 752.

2. *Id.* at 728–729.

3. Terrence W. Deacon, "Prefrontal Cortex and Symbol Learning: Why a Brain Capable of Learning Language Evolved Only Once," in *Communicating Meaning: The Evolution and Development of Language*, ed. Boris M. Velichkovsky and Duane M. Rumbaugh (Mahwah, N.J.: Lawrence Erlbaum, 1996), 105–106.

4. *Merriam-Webster's Collegiate Dictionary*, 11th ed., s.vv. "communication" and "language."

5. *See* Anna-Miria Muhlke, "The Right to Language and Linguistic Development: Deafness from a Human Rights Perspective," *Virginia Journal of International Law* 40 (2000): 705, 725.

6. *Id.* at 746–747.

7. *Id.* at 740.

8. Conversation with Dr. Rob Rosen, May 2006.

9. Muhlke, "The Right to Language and Linguistic Development," 743–744.

10. *Id.* at 752; and South African Schools Act, 1996, as provided to author by Claudine Storbeck, March 28, 2005.

11. Ross E. Mitchell and others, "How Many People Use ASL in the United States?" February 21, 2005, 25–26, http://research.gallaudet.edu/ Publications/ASL_Users.pdf.

12. *2002–2003 Regional and National Summary* (Washington, D.C.: Gallaudet Research Institute, 2003), 6.

13. Introduction to *Annual Survey of Deaf and Hard of Hearing Children & Youth* (Washington D.C.: Gallaudet Research Institute, 2000), http:// gri.gallaudet.edu/AnnualSurvey/.

14. Ross E. Mitchell and Michael A. Karchmer, "Demographics of Deaf Education: More Students in More Places," *American Annals of the Deaf* 151 (2006): 100.

15. Pamela Knight and Ruth Swanwick, *The Care and Education of a Deaf Child* (Buffalo, N.Y.: Multilingual Matters, 1999), 166.

16. John Dewey, *Philosophy and Civilization* (New York: Minton, Balch & Co., 1931), 87.

Part 2: The Argument for a Constitutional Right to Communication and Language

3

COMMUNICATION, LANGUAGE, AND EDUCATION

Language is the armory of the human mind, and at once contains the trophies of its past and the weapons of its future conquest.

—Anonymous

Joey was seven and had a profound hearing loss. For three years he had attended the state school for the deaf, where he used sign language to communicate. In the summer of 1998, Joey transferred to a school in his home school district. His IEP, which was developed before school started, called for a signing aide. School started in September, but the aide did not begin working with Joey until October. The aide was not "fluent in any sign language." In December 1998, the IEP team noted Joey's need for "increased communication" and a one-to-one communication facilitator. In May 1999, the district determined that Joey was not ready to move on to first grade. Testing showed that he was "not processing complex spoken language," and at an August 1999 meeting, his mother, aunt, and uncle all noted that he could not understand what was going on in the classroom. The uncle, who was an assistant superintendent at a school for the deaf in another state, recommended a signing aide for his nephew, which was precisely what had been on the August 1998 IEP but had never been provided.

In September 1999 a local hospital specializing in hearing loss recommended that Joey be provided the "services of a sign language facilitator to promote his understanding of classroom instruction, discussions, and interactions." Three months later the hospital recommended a signing aide fluent in Pidgin Sign English (a signing system that combines elements of ASL with English). Finally, in October 1999, more than a year after the initial IEP meeting and Joey's return to the school district, the school agreed to provide a full-time signing aide.

The new signing aide sat near Joey. When the teacher asked the students to open their reading books, the aide spoke but did not sign to

Joey, who did not move. When the teacher noticed that Joey was not ready, she waved her arms to get his attention. She held up the book and then pointed to him. For a moment, nothing happened; then he realized that the teacher wanted him to take out his book. After he placed the book on his desk, he turned to the aide and made the sign for *book*. Easily, even sweetly, he put his hands together and opened and closed them twice. The aide watched him and then repeated the sign. Her sign was not smooth—she was trying this sign for the first time. Joey took her hands and positioned them so that she could more effectively open and close them.

Fifteen minutes later, the teacher turned to the blackboard, where the numbers one through twenty were listed. As the teacher pointed to each number, she said slowly, "one . . . one . . . two . . . two . . ." The aide signed "one, two, three," all the way to twenty. The lesson lasted for ten minutes.

Testimony would later be introduced in a due process hearing that the only signs the aide knew were those Joey had taught her—and the numbers one through twenty.[1]

THE ROLE OF COMMUNICATION AND LANGUAGE IN EDUCATIONAL GROWTH

SCHOOL IS PERHAPS, more than anything else, a language laboratory. It is where linguistic skills mature and a child's sense of self and knowledge grow. Emotional, intellectual, and educational growth is unthinkable without the ability to communicate, to exchange ideas and information. Language is the linchpin of everything we learn.

It is difficult to imagine that many hearing children go to school without age-appropriate language skills or are placed in classrooms where they cannot access the language around them. Deaf and hard of hearing students, however, are often placed in educational programs that do not help them *develop* language skills or provide *access* to the language around them. Many have experiences like Joey's.

Classrooms provide a "rich source of information to children" and surround them with "interaction and modeling" that is "essential to cognitive development."[2] Access to fluent conversation is necessary for language and cognitive growth; indeed, much of a child's linguistic growth comes from interaction with peers, through the casual, ongoing interchange between children. Children learn language, whether it is spoken or signed, by "putting language to purposeful social [use]. . . . Language development is that internal cognitive and symbolic process . . . initiated and supported in local social contexts that in turn bring children into contact with the broad knowledge of their culture's conventions of language forms and uses."[3]

Of course, the process of developing language—which is necessary for educational growth—should begin before a child enters school. Approximately 95 percent of deaf children lose their hearing before they develop language, and about 90 percent of deaf children have hearing parents.[4] It is not surprising, then, that many deaf children lose valuable time in developing language, making language-rich educational environments that much more important. Early identification is critical; Christine Yoshinaga-Itano and Mah-Rya Apuzzo have found that children whose hearing loss is identified between birth and six months have three times more receptive and expressive language than those whose hearing loss is identified between seven and eighteen months.[5] But regardless of a child's language skill level when he or she enters school, school is central to continued linguistic and educational growth.

A deaf or hard of hearing child's ability to develop age-appropriate linguistic as well as cognitive and literacy skills is directly related to the quality of the language instruction, not necessarily the kind of language or the communication mode. Deaf and hard of hearing people develop the ability to read, think, and succeed academically because they have language, not because they have a certain language. Deaf and hard of hearing children have the same range of innate abilities that hearing children do and have the same ability to develop language. Indeed, deaf and hard of hearing children's ability to learn sign language underlines "the biological capacity that young children possess for developing language whatever its modalities." Grammatical development in signing children parallels that in children using spoken language, and deaf children with a deaf parent "are able to acquire fluency in sign language at the same rate as hearing children acquire a spoken language and . . . they also go through parallel stages in their language development."[6]

Ultimately, deaf and hard of hearing children do not lack the capacity for language, only the opportunity to develop it. That is the issue before us, and it is one that requires special protection. Language access and development is that important.

Delayed or incomplete language development and a barren language environment have serious consequences for a child's ability to learn to read. Statistics reveal coldly but clearly that reading skills suffer when a child does not have language or the school system does not provide for language development and access. For the last thirty years, the reading scores of deaf and hard of hearing high school seniors have remained between third- and fourth-grade levels (hearing eighteen-year-olds generally score at the tenth-grade reading level); 30 percent leave school functionally illiterate, and even those who go on to college have significant literacy problems.[7]

None of the standardized assessment tools are able to provide information to compare a deaf or hard of hearing child's chronological age with his or her linguistic age. For example, we do not have statistics on how many deaf children who are, say, between eight and ten have the language skills (whether manual or aural-oral) of a four- to six-year-old child or an eight- to ten-year-old child.* But we do know that in the late 1990s, 8 percent of deaf and hard of hearing students graduated from college and that deaf and hard of hearing children between the ages of eight and eighteen gained only 1.5 years in reading skills.[8] In 2000, 75 percent

---

*I have asked individuals at Gallaudet University and other institutions about this, and no one has been able to point to an assessment tool that would provide vital information about a deaf or hard of hearing child's level of language ability relative to his or her age.

of deaf students in Colorado performed in the "unsatisfactory, partially proficient range."[9]

Failed language development and failed education soon lead to compromised adult lives. Almost one-third of all deaf adults rely on some form of governmental assistance, and the average income of deaf adults is 40 to 60 percent of that of their hearing counterparts. Approximately 40 percent of deaf adults are unemployed, and 90 percent are underemployed.[10]

So although language access and development are central to educational and human growth, two essential factors are missing for deaf and hard of hearing students: access to the rich language environment of the classroom and programs that help them develop age-appropriate language and communication skills.

LACK OF ACCESS TO A LANGUAGE-RICH ENVIRONMENT

Deaf and hard of hearing students attend a variety of school programs. Some are mainstreamed and are likely to be the only deaf or hard of hearing students in their classes or schools. Some go to state schools where there are many other deaf students as well as deaf teachers who use sign language. Still others are placed in special programs where there may be some other deaf or hard of hearing students, but perhaps of different ages and cognitive abilities and likely to use very different communication modes. Finally, many attend special-education classes in which students are hearing and autistic, developmentally delayed, or behaviorally or emotionally troubled. Thus many deaf and hard of hearing students are cut off from language and communication in school because

1. the staff cannot communicate directly with the students;*
2. there are insufficient or no support services to ensure ac-

---

*There is no federal law (and I am unaware of any state law) that requires a teacher who works with deaf and hard of hearing students—whether in regular or special-education settings—to demonstrate a specific level of sign language skill.

cess, including qualified interpreters, note takers, and the like;

3. there is a small or nonexistent peer population with whom the students can communicate directly and easily;

4. communication between deaf and hard of hearing students and hearing students in regular or special-education classes is minimal and usually stagnant;

5. whether as a result of law or policy, school districts discourage, restrict, or deny placement in language-rich environments like a center or state school that has staff proficient in the deaf or hard of hearing child's language or a critical mass of language, age, and cognitive peers;

6. schools lack expertise regarding the important role of acoustics and the importance of hearing aids, cochlear implants, and FM systems, and few schools have staff trained to work with hard of hearing students;

7. many classrooms and facilities are acoustically inappropriate;

8. there are no language specialists to help children develop their language skills, whether in spoken English, ASL, or written English; and

9. few schools have programs to assist deaf and hard of hearing children in developing skills in signing systems, Cued Speech, and other communication options.

The range of missing elements for deaf and hard of hearing students in the educational system is present, to a greater or lesser degree, in all placement options, including state schools. We can look more carefully at programs in which language access is limited because of a lack of services (qualified interpreters), a lack of peer interaction opportunities, and a lack of language-proficient staff, since the missing elements are indeed more apparent. Generally, this happens more frequently in regular or special-education classes in local school districts. This is not to suggest that one placement is better than another; after all, parents have the right to determine where their child can be best served. But the statistics regarding placement reveal a good deal about the paucity of language these placements provide.

As of 2003, 79,556 students in the United States between the ages of three and twenty-two had a hearing loss.[11] Given the variety of communication and language options for deaf and hard of hearing children and the singularly important issue of developing and accessing language, the program options available reflect the structural difficulties these children face right from the beginning.

Historically, deaf children attended state schools for the deaf, but with the passage of the IDEA in 1975 and its preference for placing children with disabilities in regular, or mainstreamed, classes, more and more deaf and hard of hearing children were placed in regular classes or special day classes. They were removed from the state-school environment, where there were teachers who were deaf, hearing teachers with proficient signing skills, and a critical mass of signing peers.

In 1975, approximately 20,000 deaf and hard of hearing students attended state residential schools for the deaf; by 1993, that number had dropped to 9,855. During that same period, placements in integrated classes increased 148 percent.[12] By 2002, only 4,838 were enrolled in state schools, and 30,000 deaf and hard of hearing students in the United States spent 80 percent or more of their time in a regular classroom.[13] But the increase in regular school placements did not result in more language opportunities. On the contrary, the students who left the residential schools also left behind their language peers, and they found themselves in schools where there were only a few deaf students. Between 1979 and 1986, the number of programs with only one deaf or hard of hearing student increased nationally from 1,797 to 4,412.[14] The issue is not whether a state school or a local program is best; it is, more importantly, the language consequences of any specific placement.

In 1997, 360 of California's 500 school districts reported serving fewer than ten deaf students. One-half of the school districts in New York had between zero and ten deaf students. In Alabama, 24 out of 35 school districts had ten or fewer deaf students. Even in those districts that had a dozen or more deaf children, the age distribution minimized the chances that a student would have age and language peers in any one class or even in school.[15] There is of course no easy answer to this problem; the First and Fourteenth Amendments are not capable of changing population distribution. The reality is that the educational environment for many deaf children provides few if any true language peers, little or no access to the actual language around them, and little or no socialization and interaction—all the basis for language development. This triple impact is devastating in terms of linguistic, psychological, emotional, and social growth—not to mention cognitive and academic development. One deaf woman who attended public schools for her entire K–12 education describes her experience as follows:

> When I try to remember . . . I see myself walking alone.
> . . . I see myself walking into my homeroom, feeling self-conscious. I see myself gathering up my books quickly whenever the bell rang, going directly to my next class.
> . . . I never talked to anyone. . . . For [deaf and hard of hearing children] the loneliness and lack of self-esteem resulting from the pervasive feeling of being different and left out were so damaging as to negate any academic benefit.[16]

For those students who are placed in special classes in regular or special schools, the lack of linguistic access is significant, including

1. a considerable age span (in some cases, ten years may separate one deaf or hard of hearing child from another deaf or nondeaf classmate);
2. cross-categorical grouping of deaf and hard of hearing students with no additional disabilities with autistic, learning

disabled, and developmentally delayed hearing students; and
3. significant cognitive and linguistic differences between the students in classes in which deaf or hard of hearing children are placed.[17]

Imagine placing an eight-year-old English-speaking hearing child in a class where the students range in age from five to eighteen, where 90 percent of the other children speak only Russian, and where few, if any, of the other children have the same cognitive abilities as the English-speaking child. Throw in a couple of students with severe behavioral problems and a few more with autism, and you have a scenario not uncommon for deaf and hard of hearing children.

Helen Keller said that "blindness cuts people off from things, deafness cuts people off from people"; others have expanded that to mean that the "essential problem of deafness is not a lack of hearing but an abundance of isolation." Not surprisingly, the "most effective way to address problems of deafness would be to increase the critical mass of interpersonal and informational opportunities" available to deaf and hard of hearing children.[18] If so many deaf and hard of hearing children do not have access to this critical mass, then alternatives must be found to increase their opportunities to communicate with their peers, because "participation in interactions with others is not the only factor that leads a child to construct knowledge and theories of how people and things operate. . . . Cognitive development is *the product* of sociocultural *interaction*, mediated by language."[19]

The "quality of peer relationships" has "emerged as a consistent predictor of maladjustment in adolescence and adulthood."[20] Socialization between peers happens throughout the day, involves subtle and complex interactions between children, and requires a kind of privacy that allows children and adolescents to communicate freely among themselves. Thus, again, if language is a prerequisite for socialization as well as academic and cognitive growth, the *quality* of language access is equally important and the placement options become critical for deaf and hard of hearing children.

Researchers have found that not only are the communications between deaf and hearing children highly limited, but they reflect unequal roles in which the hearing children view their deaf and hard of hearing peers as inferior and in need of caretaking rather than as friends of equal status. Elizabeth Keating and Gene Mirus observed the following:

1. Deaf children spent long periods of time as nonparticipants in peer interaction, having neither direct communication nor even peripheral involvement (e.g., standing in a group and "listening" to language but not necessarily participating directly).
2. When deaf and hearing students did communicate, the interactions were shorter, more limited, and static.
3. Most of the interactions focused on current topics. Few conversations had past or future context, which is necessary for a rich and normal language world. Thus, in the lunchroom, for example, language exchanges between deaf and hearing students were limited to the most perfunctory matters of what was being eaten, what time it was, and the like.
4. Hearing students used few signs, which further limited the normal language exchange between peers. Keating and Mirus noted that "if schools are assuming that deaf students are learning through interacting with hearing peers" they are mistaken, because the interactions were "notable for their lack of real language."[21]

Keating and Mirus concluded that "what most deaf children lack is not engagement with the hearing world, but engagement with competent peer visual language producers. . . . They were not linguistically assimilated."[22] Their findings are consistent with other findings that mainstreaming may very well lead to a greater sense of marginalization, higher levels of stress, and impairment in physical and psychological well-being.[23] Ironically and unfortunately, "most deaf children are expected to acquire a spoken language first—perhaps English—despite the fact that they are acutely detached from the English-speaking community and may never be able to join it fully."[24]

The hearing world and the hearing education system sometimes mistake the ability to sign one's name or sign "Hello, how are you?" as true communication. Because of the lack of acoustically appropriate rooms, of staff trained to teach students with limited hearing, and of necessary support services, the language limitations are equally profound for those deaf and hard of hearing students who are primarily oral-aural. Gina A. Oliva, a professor at Gallaudet University, has written a vivid and compelling book about the experiences of deaf and hard of hearing students, aptly titled *Alone in the Mainstream*. Oliva, who describes herself as the "only child with a hearing loss in all the schools" she attended between kindergarten and the twelfth grade, writes of her reaction to the ongoing placement of deaf and hard of hearing students, oral and signing, in regular classrooms where language access is severely limited. She despairs at the thought that the generations after her "will have to go through what I went through."[25]

THE COMPLEX ISSUE OF INTERPRETED EDUCATION

The use of sign language interpreters adds an additional complicating factor to the important issue of language access for deaf and hard of hearing children.[26] Joey's experience is not uncommon—interpreted education, even at its best, reflects a difficult linguistic compromise. Yet despite its inherent limitations, an interpreted education provides an absolute lifeline to deaf and hard of hearing students, something that was denied to Amy Rowley, the only deaf child in a hearing school (see chapter 1). Because interpreters represent the single most significant and common avenue for language access, some key issues need to be examined in light of the constitutional right argued here.

- Since there is no absolute right to a sign language interpreter, the question arises as to whether the school will agree that the student needs one. The IDEA lists a sign language interpreter as a related service, but, as in the case of any such service, the IEP team must agree on its provision, a matter subject to yearly debate and disagreement.
- School systems do not require that sign language interpreters be certified, and, not surprisingly, the quality of interpreters can vary greatly. Joey's interpreter is not an anomaly.
- Because of pay and other related factors, even a school that wants to provide an interpreter may have difficulty finding one, qualified or not.
- Even certified interpreters understand only 57 percent of what is signed in ASL, and noncertified interpreters understand 29 percent of what is signed. This means that, at best, they are vocalizing only 29 to 57 percent of what the deaf or hard of hearing child signs in ASL, thus seriously compromising two-way communication.[27]
- In a 2004 study of 1,300 interpreters, all had difficulty with prosody—those elements of language that mark lexical and grammatical boundaries and provide cues to linguistic division.[28]
- In 2000, almost 90 percent of the interpreters in Oregon were not certified, and 81 percent of West Virginia's K–12 educational interpreters had no certification.[29]

Studies show that deaf students who have interpreters are "not genuine participants in the hearing classroom" and that their interactions with peers and teachers are "impoverished." By contrast, when deaf students communicate directly with each other, the discussions are complex, "about abstract thoughts, arguments, and negotiations, and metalinguistic discussions."[30]

In addition to the provision of qualified, let alone any, interpreters, there is the issue of an adult intermediary for a student. We know that an interpreted education—often referred to as a *mediated process*—involves the constant presence of an adult literally and figuratively placed between the deaf child and that child's peers and teachers. This has obvious limitations on classroom and social interchanges, which are exacerbated by the lag time between the spoken and interpreted statement. The following story is a perfect illustration.

> All of the eleventh-graders are speaking or listening, directly or indirectly. Except for one student, sitting down in front. She is neither speaking nor listening; she is not involved; she is deaf.
>
> I am her sign language interpreter. I stand in front of the class, poised to begin signing whenever she looks at me, but she doesn't; she is resting her eyes on the sky outside the window. When at last she does turn her face, it is not to see what her classmates are saying but to chat with me about her weekend, about the book I am reading, about her dog, my sweater, anything. She is hungry for communication and chooses me—an adult satellite paid to follow her through the school day—rather than her peers, who do not speak her language.
>
> Class begins. She pays attention for a while. Sometimes when the teacher asks a question, she signs a response, which I interpret into spoken English—always a little late, just a few seconds after the other students. Sometimes the students will talk at once; their voices overlap and I have to choose one thread to follow, or compress them all in a quick synopsis, inserting who said which thing to whom and in what tone of voice.[31]

Given the initial limitations of interpreted education, certainly when it is provided it is essential that it be of the highest quality. One has to wonder whether deaf and hard of hearing children are receiving educational opportunities equal to those of their peers, as has been required for more than fifty years under *Brown v. Board of Education*. Even if an interpreted education does not provide the optimum language environment, it is the only way to make linguistic access available to deaf and hard of hearing students. However, the truth is that there are not enough interpreters, too many of them are not qualified or certified, and school systems are not willing to provide the necessary resources to improve the interpreter pool, which makes an already difficult situation untenable.

If language *access* is fundamental, its companion is language *development*. Just as it is the responsibility of families and schools to teach basic reading skills, it is up to both to ensure that all children, including deaf and hard of hearing children, have age-appropriate language skills. Currently, though, no state or federal law requires school districts to provide services and programs that focus on language development. To assume that these children will become literate and academically skilled without language is like assuming children will become adept at algebra without understanding basic arithmetic. I would argue that failing to provide language development—whether that means ASL, signing systems, or aural-oral language development—is the same as, if not worse than, a school system systemically failing to provide a reading program to all hearing children.

Accordingly, our schools must, in conjunction with families and other institutions responsible for the welfare of our nation's children, determine the language skill level of every deaf and hard of hearing child, develop a specific, ongoing, and formal program to help the child develop his or her unique communication mode and language (whether oral-aural, ASL, or a signing system), and monitor these programs to ensure that each child has a fair and appropriate opportunity for language development.

When the issue of teacher competency comes up in this nation, the debate is often serious and the subsequent changes significant. The passage of the No Child Left Behind Act (NCLB) and its requirement that teachers demonstrate necessary competency is just one example of how our political bodies act with some alacrity when such basic educational matters arise (whether the NCLB is effective or whether the further "quantification" of education is sound is another matter). There is little doubt that parents in this nation would not tolerate or even understand an educational program in which their hearing children could not communicate with staff or peers. That this is tolerated for deaf and hard of hearing children is inexcusable; thus, the call for a constitutional recognition of the right to communication and language is justified and timely.

NOTES

1. *In re West Central Indiana Special Education Services*, 32 I.D.E.L.R. (LRP) § 249, at 828 (Ind. Bd. Special Educ. Appeals 2000).

2. Brenda Schick, "How Might Learning through an Educational Interpreter Influence Cognitive Development?" in *Educational Interpreting: How It Can Succeed*, ed. Elizabeth A. Winston (Washington, D.C.: Gallaudet University Press, 2004), 74.

3. Claire L. Ramsey, *Deaf Children in Public Schools: Placement, Context, and Consequences* (Washington, D.C.: Gallaudet University Press, 2002), 6–7.

4. Commission on Education of the Deaf, *Toward Equality: Education of the Deaf; A Report to the President and Congress of the United States* (Washington, D.C.: Government Printing Office, 1988), 15.

5. Christine Yoshinaga-Itano and Mah-Rya L. Apuzzo, "The Development of Deaf and Hard of Hearing Children Identified Early through the High-Risk Registry," *American Annals of the Deaf* 143 (1998): 416, 421–423.

6. Pamela Knight and Ruth Swanwick, *The Care and Education of a Deaf Child* (Buffalo: Multilingual Matters, 1999), 94, 101.

7. Marc Marschark, *Raising and Educating a Deaf Child* (New York: Oxford University Press, 1997), 135–136.

8. Lawrence Siegel, "The Educational and Communication Needs of Deaf and Hard of Hearing Children," *American Annals of the Deaf* 145 (2000): 64–77.

9. Colorado Department of Education, Exceptional Student Services, *Colorado Quality Standards* (Colorado Department of Education, 2004), 5, http://www.cde.state.co.us/cdesped/download/pdf/colorado_quality_standards2004.pdf.

10. Commission on Education of the Deaf, *Toward Equality*, 17.

11. U.S. Department of Education, *To Assure the Free Appropriate Public Education of All Children with Disabilities: Twenty-fifth Annual Report to Congress on the Implementation of the Individuals with Disabilities Education Act, 2003* (Washington, D.C., 2003), AA7.

12. Arthur N. Schildroth and Sue A. Hotto, "Deaf Students and Full Inclusion: Who Wants to be Excluded?" in *Implications and Complications for Deaf Students of the Full Inclusion Movement*, ed. Oscar Cohen and Robert C. Johnson (Washington, D.C.; Gallaudet Research Institute, 1994), 20.

13. U.S. Department of Education, Office of Special Education and Rehabilitative Services, *Twenty-sixth Annual Report to Congress on the Implementation of the Individuals with Disabilities Education Act, 2004* (Washington, D.C., 2004), 165 (table 2–2f).

14. Arthur Schildroth, "Recent Changes in the Educational Placement of Deaf Students," *American Annals of the Deaf* 133 (1988): 61–62.

15. Siegel, "Educational and Communication Needs," 16.

16. Gina A. Oliva, *Alone in the Mainstream* (Washington, D.C.: Gallaudet University Press, 2004), 75.

17. Commission on Education of the Deaf, *Toward Equality*, 28–29.

18. Harold A. Johnson, "U.S. Deaf Education Teacher Preparation Programs: A Look at the Present and Vision of the Future," *American Annals of the Deaf* 149 (2004): 76.

19. Schick, "Learning through an Educational Interpreter," 74 (emphasis added).

20. Michael Stinson and Harry Lang, "The Potential Impact on Deaf Students of the Full Inclusion Movement" in *Implications and Complications for Deaf Students of the Full Inclusion Movement*, ed. Oscar Cohen and Robert C. Johnson (Washington, D.C.: Gallaudet Research Institute, 1994), 33.

21. Elizabeth Keating and Gene Mirus, "Examining Interactions across

Language Modalities: Deaf Children and Hearing Peers at School," *Anthropology & Education Quarterly* 34 (2003): 129–131.

22. *Id.* at 131.

23. *See, e.g.*, "Acculturative Stress: A Useful Framework for Understanding the Experience of Deaf Americans," Robert G. Brubaker, *JADARA* 28, no. 1 (1994): 1–16.

24. Ramsey, *Deaf Children in Public Schools*, 8.

25. Oliva, *Alone in the Mainstream*, 1, 3.

26. A full analysis of interpreted education is beyond the scope of this book. See *Educational Interpreting: How It Can Succeed*, edited by Elizabeth Winston (Washington, D.C.: Gallaudet University Press, 2002), for just one of many books on this subject.

27. Christine Monikowski, "Language Myths in Interpreted Education: First Language, Second Language, What Language?" in *Educational Interpreting: How It Can Succeed*, ed. Elizabeth A. Winston (Washington, D.C.: Gallaudet University Press, 2004), 51.

28. Schick, "Learning through an Educational Interpreter," 77.

29. Bernhardt E. Jones, "Competencies of K–12 Educational Interpreters: What We Need versus What We Have," in *Educational Interpreting: How It Can Succeed*, ed. Elizabeth A. Winston (Washington, D.C.: Gallaudet University Press, 2004), 116–117.

30. Schick, "Learning through an Educational Interpreter," 75.

31. Leah Hager Cohen, Op-Ed., "Schools for All, or Separate But Equal?" *New York Times*, February 22, 1994.

THE FIRST AMENDMENT:
THE BROAD RIGHT TO EXPRESS AND
RECEIVE INFORMATION AND IDEAS

Without free speech no search for truth is possible, without free speech no discovery of truth is useful. . . . Better a thousandfold abuse of free speech than a denial of free speech. The abuse dies in a day, but the denial slays the life of the people.

—Charles Bradlaugh

The school administrator turned to the parents, smiled, and said, "I just want the best for your child."

They didn't doubt it, but the problem was in the details. Debra was eleven; she had a cochlear implant, could hear sounds, and in a quiet environment, could distinguish language. She was of average intelligence and was at grade level in basic skill development. The school district had placed her in a special day class for deaf and hard of hearing students in which the students used both sign language and oral-aural language. The students ranged in age from six to fourteen, and their cognitive abilities varied widely. On any given day Debra might be sitting next to a six-year-old who communicated exclusively through sign language or a fourteen-year-old who had aural-oral skills but the cognitive abilities of a four-year-old.

The program had a teacher qualified to work with deaf and hard of hearing students, a full-time but noncertified sign language interpreter, and a part-time speech pathologist who worked with Debra and her classmates, three hours a week, on recognizing spoken language and enhancing their ability to speak. This work was exhausting, and Debra made slow progress. The special day class was twenty-five miles from her home, and although school started at 8 a.m., she had to catch a bus at 6:30 a.m. School ended at 3 p.m., but Debra did not get home until 5:30 p.m.

"We appreciate your position here," the parents said, "but our daughter is in the wrong program. How would you like it if your child was in a class where there were children five years older and five years younger? We want her to go to her neighborhood school just as her brother did, just as all her friends do."

The administrator responded, "If Debra attends Washington Elementary, she would need her own individual speech pathologist; do you think it is fair that every deaf child in our district have his or her own individual speech pathologist?"

The parents replied, "We don't know about that. Debra is a kid. She's eleven years old, and she wants to go to school with her neighborhood friends. She wants to be in a class with other eleven-year-olds and not with fourteen-year-olds or six-year-olds. She wants to be in a place where she can better develop her oral and aural abilities."

"I am sorry, but we disagree here. I have a duty to Debra but also to other students, and it will cost this district an additional $55,000 to $70,000 a year just to hire a personal speech pathologist for Debra. It will then cost us many thousands of dollars to put rugs into her classrooms and add acoustical tiles. I can't do that and not harm the other children in this district. And I won't. She is doing well, and the law does give us some flexibility in placing her in the program she is currently in. I'm sorry, but if we have to go to a hearing on this one, and even to court, I am fully prepared to do so."

The administrator paused. She had been in a thousand IEP meetings, a hundred mediations, and dozens of due process hearings. She had worked with all kinds of children, had in fact been a speech therapist before she got her administrator's credential. She was sure she understood deaf and hard of hearing children as well as she understood autistic and emotionally troubled kids.

"She'll never learn to function in a hearing world if her hand is held every day of her life. I know it's hard, but Debra is a very strong young lady, and she will be better equipped to go out into the hearing world with the help she is getting in her special day class. In that regular class at Washington, she'll slip further behind." The administrator began to gather her papers, but added, "Someone has to look out for this child's well-being."

Because Debra's school district refused to agree to her placement in her home school, the family hired an attorney. They spent almost $5,000 for the attorney to review the case and attend a mediation meeting with the school district. Although the attorney vigorously argued that Debra had an educational and legal right to attend her neighborhood school, the mediation was not binding and the school district would not change its position.

Several days after the mediation, the attorney explained the options that remained for Debra and her family. An administrative hearing would cost at least an additional $5,000. If Debra's parents won, the district would have to reimburse them for the legal costs; if they lost, they would have to pay for their own legal costs. They asked what their chances of success were. "No more than 50/50 and probably a little less," the attorney replied. Debra's right to be educated with her hearing peers and in her home school was offset by many decisions in which the courts had sided with the school districts when the cost of placing a child in a regular class was high.

Debra's parents mentioned that they thought cost was not supposed to be a factor under the IDEA's "free appropriate public education" rule. The attorney indicated that it shouldn't be, but then explained, "Here's what the officer or the judge is thinking. 'This student is in a good program, she's doing well, she has a qualified teacher of the deaf and hard of hearing and a good speech pathologist, and you want this district to spend thousands of dollars to place her in her neighborhood school?'"

"But how would that judge feel if it were his child?" the parents asked.

The attorney shrugged. "You're right, but whether we like it or not, you have as much of a chance of losing as winning. And if you lose and appeal the hearing to a court, the additional cost will be at least $10,000 and likely a lot more. And if we win at the hearing or at the first level of court, the district can appeal that decision all the way to the Supreme Court. The cost would be significant. If you ultimately win, the school will have to pay for all your legal fees, but if you eventually lose—"

Debra's parents asked whether they would have to go through this same process every year for the next seven to eight years of Debra's school life. The attorney was direct. "If you win, probably not, although there is no guarantee, since this school district has a track record of being very aggressive in these matters. If you lose, yes."

Six weeks later Debra's parents began to look for a school district that was more flexible about mainstreaming deaf and hard of hearing children, especially those with cochlear implants. Three months later, they uprooted their family from a city they had lived in for thirteen years and moved two hundred miles east.

THE DEVALUATION OF COMMUNICATION AND LANGUAGE UNDER THE IDEA

PARENTS LOSE AS OFTEN as they win when they are forced to battle for communication access. In *Board of Education v. Rowley*, the U.S. Supreme Court ruled unequivocally that a child had no right under the IDEA to a particular program or "methodology." Vital communication and language is reduced to something routine, secondary. Other courts have taken up the limiting "methodology" position.

In referring to methodology, the Supreme Court was not discussing a difference in reading strategies or varying methods of working with autistic children, but rather whether a deaf or hard of hearing child would be placed in an educational environment in which that child would be able to access the flow of information. Access to communication—the essence of our First Amendment right—is for deaf and hard of hearing children merely something that educators, not the child or his or her family, can choose, just as they might choose one biography about Thomas Jefferson over another. But the First Amendment right to access information in a classroom cannot merely be a "methodology" dispute.

That a court might not understand why a parent is entitled to demand that his or her child have access to language and therefore information is remarkable and troubling. Debra, Joey, and Amy Rowley have a fundamental right to access the "flow of information" in their classrooms, whether through a qualified interpreter or through a language aide. The First Amendment to our Constitution guarantees this right, and although no court has considered it when analyzing the so-called methodology issue of language and communication, it is time that our most precious right apply to deaf and hard of hearing children.

THE BROAD NATURE OF THE FIRST AMENDMENT

The First Amendment provides, "Congress shall make no law respecting an establishment of religion, or prohibiting the free exercise thereof; or abridging the freedom of speech, or of the press, or the right of the people peaceably to assemble, and to petition the Government for a redress of grievances."[1]

Consider the diversity of communication that occurs in an American classroom: topics may include John F. Kennedy's assassination, the debate about evolution, the Pythagorean theorem, global warming, September 11, prayer in school, the principal's decision to cancel a school dance, the requirement to do extra sit-ups in gym class, the capitals of European countries, and a thousand other matters. Is there another place in American society where there is a more important flow of information? The free flow of information, which is at the heart of our democracy, is the challenge and joy of American education.

Think of democracy and many think of the First Amendment before anything else. It gives us the right to know, the right to express and receive information and ideas. Of course, this right is subject to restrictions, but we are not analyzing here the edges of the First Amendment; rather, we are considering the underlying notion that once knowledge, thought, and ideas are available to a group of students, they must be available to all, even deaf children. Yet deaf and hard of hearing children are denied this right in many different ways.

- A child may be denied the chance to go to a language-rich school where direct communication with peers and teachers is possible.
- A school may fail to provide a language-proficient teacher.
- A child may not understand most or all of what the teacher tells the class.
- A student may not be able to communicate with his or her

peers or teacher because there is no qualified interpreter to facilitate that interchange.

◆ A child who relies on oral-aural communication may not receive the support necessary to understand classroom speech.

◆ The daily announcements, discussions, assemblies, debates, and other exchanges, both large and small, may be unavailable to a student.

The child who is denied the right in school to learn about communism or evolution or the novels of Charles Dickens or whatever topic may have gained contemporary currency is denied much. Deaf and hard of hearing children who are denied access to communication itself are denied everything. The flow of information in a classroom, which represents our participation in our democracy, hovers about every child but the deaf child. The lack of access to a language-rich environment deprives the deaf or hard of hearing child of the linguistic tools necessary to participate in the classroom and, accordingly, our democracy.

By restricting the exchange of information, schools are robbing these children of the free interchange of ideas, for "if the opinion [being debated] is right, they are deprived of the opportunity of exchanging error for truth; if wrong, they lose, what is almost as great a benefit, the clearer perception and livelier impression of truth produced by its collision with error."[2]

FREEDOM TO COMMUNICATE: A BROADER RIGHT THAN FREEDOM OF SPEECH

Human beings do not like to be told that they cannot say their piece or access what others think. This is not a new thing. In the fifth century B.C.E., Herodotus said, "It is clear that not in one thing alone, but in many ways, equality and freedom of speech are a good thing."[3] More than two thousand years later, the Supreme Court justice William O. Douglas bluntly declared that freedom of speech is "not to be regulated like diseased cattle and impure butter."[4] Freedom of speech is made greater because we, or most of us, don't have to think about its absence.

The right to speak freely is the right to be free, and American history is rife with examples of how Americans have challenged and upheld this right. George Washington understood that "freedom of speech may be taken away, and, dumb and silent, we may be led, like sheep, to the Slaughter."[5] When Franklin Roosevelt articulated his four essential human freedoms, the first was freedom of speech. This basic freedom has "contributed greatly to the development and well-being of our free society and [is] indispensable to its continued growth. Ceaseless vigilance is the watchword to prevent [its] erosion by Congress or by the States."[6]

However, by focusing on the phrase *freedom of speech*, we ironically narrow its true constitutional parameters. Freedom of speech is a subset of a larger and more significant human condition and right: the ability to convey and receive information. When the U.S. Supreme Court ruled that a public school could not ban the works of Richard Wright or Kurt Vonnegut from its library[7] and that another school could not prevent a student from wearing an armband protesting the Vietnam War,[8] it recognized the broader meaning of free speech to include the free exchange of information, no matter how it is conveyed.

Speech is defined as "the communication or expression of thoughts in spoken words." *Communication* is defined as "a process by which information is exchanged between individuals through a common system of symbols, signs, or behavior."[9] Speech is subsumed under the broader notion of communication, and the right to free communication is the overarching privilege. As the constitutional scholar Alexander Meiklejohn wrote, "The First Amendment is not, in the first instance, concerned with the 'right' of the speaker to this or that. It is concerned with the authority of the hearers to meet together, to discuss, and to hear discussion by speakers."[10]

Meiklejohn's use of the terms *hearers* and *to hear* does not exclude deaf and hard of hearing children from the Constitution. He is discussing here not the mode of communication but the right to access it: "The primary purpose of the First Amendment is, then, that all the citizens shall, so far as possible, understand the issues which bear upon our common life. *That is why no idea, no opinion, no doubt, no belief, no counter belief, no relevant information may be kept from them.*"[11] One doubts Meiklejohn would find access to only 60 percent of those ideas, opinions, doubts, beliefs, and counterbeliefs acceptable under the First Amendment.

Meiklejohn understood what our highest court has recognized as central to our individual and national well-being, namely, that the First Amendment "embraces at least the liberty to discuss publicly and truthfully all matters of public concern without previous restraint."[12] So it is the denial of access to information that is the most damaging. This applies powerfully and directly to deaf and hard of hearing children, who, in asserting a constitutional right to communication and language, are asking for what the rest of us take for granted—the right to receive those ideas, doubts, beliefs, and the counterbeliefs of which Meiklejohn spoke. Even if we accept that the First Amendment has limitations, as Justice Oliver Wendell Holmes asserted when he wrote that "the most stringent protection of free speech would not protect a man in falsely shouting fire in a theatre and causing a panic,"[13] what is both available and denied should be available and denied equally to all children.

In 1943, the Supreme Court ruled that a Struthers, Ohio, ordinance that prevented individuals from distributing information by ringing doorbells or knocking on doors violated the First Amendment. In his opinion, Justice Black wrote, "The right of freedom of speech . . . has broad scope. The authors of the First Amendment knew that novel and unconventional ideas might disturb the complacent, but they chose to encourage a freedom which they believed essential if vigorous enlightenment was ever to triumph over slothful ignorance."[14]

This freedom embraces "the right *to distribute*, the right *to receive* the right, *to read*."[15]* Here is the essence of the First Amendment. The deaf or hard of hearing child who is denied the services of a qualified interpreter is cut off from the discourse of the school day and has a barrier placed between him and the First Amendment as surely as the Struthers, Ohio, ordinance prevented the Jehovah's Witness from circulating (expressing) information and the citizens from receiving it. Yet the Supreme Court denied this right to Amy Rowley and, curiously, never raised the First Amendment issue.[16]

THE FREE FLOW OF INFORMATION IN SCHOOLS

The right to express and receive information and ideas has a direct and necessary relationship with education, for "public education is the basic tool for shaping democratic values."[17] The free flow of information in education, in turn, touches upon virtually every significant component of our society. Through education, we preserve "an individual's opportunity to compete successfully in the economic marketplace."[18] Without the right "to inquire, to study and to evaluate . . . our civilization will stagnate and die."[19] It is fundamental to our right and duty to vote. It is essential as a guard against ignorance and harm. When we discuss the First Amend-

*In *Lamont v. Postmaster General,* 381 U.S. 301(1965), the U.S. Supreme Court ruled that a postal rule preventing the delivery of Communist political propaganda violated the First Amendment. In another Jehovah's Witness case, the high court reversed the imprisonment of Alma Lovell for distributing religious leaflets without a permit, because the circulation of information is basic to our liberties. Over and over, the Court has stressed the receptive nature of the First Amendment's reach and the "exercise of the freedom of communicating information and disseminating opinion." *Valentine v. Chrestensen,* 316 U.S. 52, 54 (1942). Governments may not "abridge the individual liberties" of those "who wish to speak, write, print, or circulate information or opinion." *Schneider v. New Jersey,* 308 U.S. 147, 160 (1939).

ment and its availability in the American classroom, we speak of course of two kinds of communication and language. The first type is the multilayered, everyday flow of information, including lectures, announcements, and discussions in the hallway. The second type is the communication and language not available in the school, the pictures and words that are deemed inappropriate. There is, of course, much debate about what should and what should not to be discussed or read in our schools, but the lines are eventually drawn and certain items are determined to be outside the protection of the First Amendment. I do not propose here a right for deaf and hard of hearing children beyond that provided all other children; they should have the same right to access and discuss information as the other students.

So what is the nature of this important and prescribed right? In *Tinker v. Des Moines Independent Community School District*, the school district prohibited the wearing of armbands as a protest to the Vietnam War. The students and their families sued under the First Amendment, and the U.S. Supreme Court, in upholding the students' right to wear the armbands, reaffirmed that freedom of speech is the freedom to communicate in many forms, including symbolic ones. That the sentiments reflected in the words or symbols might be popular or unpopular was not the issue; rather, the Court asserted that "the vigilant protection of constitutional freedoms is nowhere more vital than in the community of American schools[,] . . . the 'marketplace of ideas'," where there must be robust exchange of ideas.[20] And it is within this powerful notion that the 40 percent of communication lost to Amy Rowley becomes more than a number.

The Court recognized that the "nation's future depends upon" such exchange and that neither students nor teachers "shed their constitutional rights to freedom of expression at the schoolhouse gate." The Court would "not confine the permissible exercise of First Amendment rights to a telephone booth or the four corners of a pamphlet, or to supervised and ordained discussion in a school classroom," and asserted that the rights included intercommunications among the students.[21] If the Supreme Court recognized that an armband is a way to convey thought, is sign language or total communication less valuable than a piece of cloth worn in protest?

In *Board of Education v. Pico*, the school board excluded Richard Wright's *Black Boy,* the poetry of Langston Hughes, and the works of Kurt Vonnegut from the school library. The U.S. Supreme Court ruled that the board's action was contrary to the First Amendment right "to receive ideas," which in turn is a "necessary predicate to the ... meaningful exercise of ... rights of speech, press, and political freedom."[23]

So we begin with a clear recognition by our Constitution and our courts that the First Amendment is about the exchange of information, that our democracy depends on that "right to know," and finally, that education and a healthy democracy are directly linked. But Amy Rowley was denied this right when the U.S. Supreme Court concluded that 60 percent of the available information was enough for her (see chapter 1 as to why she likely received much less than 60 percent). It thus becomes clear that the *Rowley-*IDEA standard—namely, that a child's needs are being met and his or her rights are being protected when that child succeeds academically—is entirely different from, and narrower than, the right to engage in the daily discussions that take place in American classrooms.*

The IDEA and the First Amendment

The IDEA is an important civil rights law. It provides unique safeguards for students with disabilities, and yet, at the same time, it

*In 2004, Congress added "oral transliteration services, cued language transliteration services, [and] sign language transliteration and interpreting services" to the IDEA. 34 C.F.R. § 300.34(c)(4)(i). But as I have noted, the provision of interpreting services depends on whether a child's parents can convince the school of the need; this most important access service is not a right. Thus *Rowley* remains the law of the land, and the case referred erects paradoxical barriers to language and communication for many deaf and hard of hearing children and ignores their First Amendment rights.

Prior to the passage of the IDEA in 1975, more than a million children with disabilities were excluded entirely from public education, and approximately four million received inappropriate educational services.[23] These children were marginalized, separated, and denied much of what constitutes an appropriate education. By 1999, there were approximately 6.1 million students with disabilities, including 80,000 deaf and hard of hearing students.[24] Federal funding for the IDEA in 2004 was $11.2 billion, which represented about 10 percent of the total cost of special education in the United States.[25]

The central purpose of the IDEA is to provide an appropriate education designed to meet a disabled child's individual needs—a free appropriate public education (FAPE)—in the least restrictive environment. The LRE requirement is a direct result of the historic segregation of students with disabilities who either were denied public-school education or were shunted off to temporary rooms at the far end of the school. This new kind of placement was called *mainstreaming*. The LRE requirement is the legitimate offspring of the movement to desegregate America, and its underlying purpose and value are unquestioned. Courts have ruled that the IDEA's "preference for mainstreaming is so strong that it might be considered as a presumptive requirement of a free appropriate public education and not merely a balancing factor."[26] Other decisions have claimed that Congress made a "clear choice among competing educational philosophies," opting for mainstreaming; the presumption that a child will be in a regular classroom is "explicit."[27]

Under the IDEA, children with disabilities, including deaf and hard of hearing children, are expected to be educated in a regular

to at the beginning of this chapter is a common one; the family must fight for the service, and even when the service is provided, it may be wholly inadequate.

classroom unless there is proof that even with the use of "supplementary aids and services" they cannot "achieve satisfactorily" in
that regular classroom.[28] Courts, including the Supreme Court in
Rowley, have ruled that children in the LRE who have the opportunity to progress in school are receiving their legal entitlements under the IDEA. Thus, although the IDEA prefers mainstreaming
and a regular classroom, the very environment that may be linguistically most challenging to many deaf and hard of hearing students,
it does not ensure First Amendment linguistic access in that environment. Language and communication become secondary to the
LRE and the FAPE requirements under the IDEA, increasing the
need for protection from other legal sources.

As discussed in chapter 2, the IDEA's LRE mandate and its
failure to value communication and language create significant difficulties for deaf and hard of hearing students and therefore raise
core First Amendment issues. The IDEA requires that the IEP
team "consider" the communication and language needs of a deaf
child, including "opportunities for direct communications with
peers and professional personnel in the child's language and communication mode . . . [and] opportunities for direct instruction in
the child's language and communication mode,"[29] but the use of
the term *consider* by Congress is not coincidental. The difference
between the requirement *to consider and discuss* and the requirement
to provide is fundamental, with clear legal implications—*shall* requires an action, but *may* and *consider* do not. In enacting the
nation's first so-called deaf child's educational bill of rights in
1993, the South Dakota legislature quite consciously avoided the
mandatory *shall*. Other states have done the same. Efforts to
change the IDEA to mandate communication and language access
have been met with resistance.

Like other IEP issues, communication and language are subject
to debate and disagreement. A deaf child's school district has absolutely no obligation to provide for the child's communication and
language needs. It has an obligation to discuss them, and that is
important, but would it be enough if a school district needed only

to discuss rather than provide a reading program for a hearing child? By not requiring communication and language access, the IDEA reinforces the weak position that communication and language play within the statutory framework. It also explains why, absent a radical change in the IDEA, deaf and hard of hearing children must look to the First Amendment for protection of the right, as the *Tinker* and *Pico* Courts ruled, to "receive ideas."

The IDEA does provide for a procedure to resolve disputes between parents and school districts. This is an important right and leaves the ultimate decision to a neutral, impartial hearing officer (or judge, if either party appeals to a state or federal court). But in any adversarial process, the parents may win, the parents may lose. For something so fundamental as communication and language and their relationship to the free flow of information, one must question whether such a need and right should be subject to the whim of an adversarial process. Would the First Amendment tolerate the provision of information to a hearing child only if the child's school team agreed she needed it? The deaf or hard of hearing child who seeks a qualified interpreter or placement in a special program faces the daunting proposition of showing that he or she is not being provided an FAPE in the least restrictive environment, even as greater constitutional rights are being ignored.

In addition, parents have the burden of showing why an ostensibly more restrictive environment—for example, the state school for the deaf, where there will be a language-rich First Amendment environment—meets the LRE requirements of the IDEA. Many language-rich environments that would ensure the First Amendment rights of deaf and hard of hearing children are presumptively disfavored under the IDEA (see chapter 2).

Since the IDEA does not mandate the provision of communication and language development, access, or opportunities for deaf and hard of hearing children, it is left to the courts to add to or subtract from the rights of these children. That parents have won some cases is hardly encouraging; that they have to go to court to secure communication and language access in the first place should be troubling. In truth, the many court decisions involving deaf and hard of hearing children and the IDEA reflect the devaluing of language and reinforce the reason the First Amendment right to a free flow of information must be forcefully applied to deaf children.

THE COURTS AND IDEA

The *Rowley* case affected all the cases that followed it, many of which have generally taken a rather dim view of the importance of communication and language. Nowhere in *Rowley* or any of these cases involving deaf children does the First Amendment make an appearance or is there a recognition of how communication and language needs are directly and dramatically related to the right to the free flow of information.

In a 1993 case, *Brougham v. Town of Yarmouth*, the parents wanted to move their nonsigning deaf son from a partially main-streamed program to the Clarke School for the Deaf in Massachu-setts. Clarke is an oral school in which the children communicate through speech and speechreading. The court ruled that it could not be considered an LRE because it was so far removed from a "regular" school environment. In deciding against the parents, the court stated that

> the Supreme Court [in *Rowley*] was . . . clear about its preference that courts not get involved in making what are primarily decisions about educational theory and *methodology*. . . . The [*Rowley*] Court clearly stated that "once a court determines that the requirements of the Act have been met, questions of methodology are for resolution by the States." . . . "*Rowley* and its progeny leave no doubt that parents, no matter how well moti-vated, do not have the right under the [IDEA] to compel a school district to provide a specific program or employ

a *specific methodology.* . . ." The only proper focus of this Court's analysis continues to be whether the proposed IEP is reasonably calculated to provide Travis with *educational benefits.*[30]

One line in the decision is significant—fatally so. A parent or child has no right to a "specific methodology." Communication and language are no longer the starting points of any educational or human endeavor, are not even remotely connected to the First Amendment, but are merely methodologies, like one particular social studies book or one strategy for teaching math.

In a 1994 case, the court refused to order a school district to provide a deaf child an interpreter for the nonacademic portions of the school day. The court said that the IDEA

> requires the school district to implement a signing system that is reasonably calculated to confer educational benefit on the hearing-impaired child. . . . [But] were we to conclude that parents could demand that their children be taught with a specific signing system, we would be creating the potential that a school district could be required to provide more than one method of signing for different students whose parents had differing preferences.[31]

The burden is on a deaf child to prove the need for an appropriate First Amendment education environment. The IDEA specifically states that a deaf or hard of hearing child can be moved to a language-rich environment in which the child can "express and receive" ideas only if "the nature or severity of the disability . . . is such that education in regular classes with the use of supplementary aids and services cannot be achieved satisfactorily."[32] Even in those cases in which the courts recognized the importance of language and ruled in favor of the child, so much time was lost in the process that the children's language and educational development was seriously compromised. In *Poolaw v. Bishop*, for example, the court ruled that an eleven-year-old deaf child who had minimal language skills (he communicated only through gestures) must go to the state school for the deaf.* Only clear evidence of utter failure renders language needs important enough to trump the IDEA's mainstreaming requirement and to bring language to the same level of importance as classroom location.

These rules could not be clearer or more devastating for many deaf or hard of hearing children. Parents must prove that the regular class is so bad that the child cannot achieve satisfactorily, even with the use of additional aids and services—a vague standard at best, difficult in reality. The burden is on the child to show why a truly rich language environment, which may not be a regular classroom, is necessary, even in light of decades of statistics that show, as noted earlier, that deaf and hard of hearing children continue to leave school functionally illiterate. The First Amendment right to express and receive ideas is a mere methodology dispute.

Deaf and hard of hearing children, like all people in this nation, are entitled to the free flow of information that makes our democracy possible. This is a right entirely separate from the IDEA and its mandates. These children should not have to go to yearly meetings to prove that right, should not have to struggle through cumbersome and costly administrative processes to secure that which is both unquestioned for all other children and central to

*There have been decisions that have recognized the importance of language for deaf and hard of hearing children. See *Visco v. School District*, 684 F. Supp. 1310, 1316 (W.D. Pa. 1988), in which the court asserted that "mainstreaming that interferes with the acquisition of fundamental language skills is foolishness mistaken for wisdom." In *Poolaw v. Bishop*, 67 F.3d 830, 837 (9th Cir. 1995), the court ruled in favor a school district's request to place a deaf child in the Arizona School for the Deaf and Blind because he specifically needed an ASL "language-rich environment" with students "his own age" who have "similar language skills" and who are "constantly using sign language."

any educational growth. The rights of these children must be joined to the First Amendment to our Constitution.

NOTES

1. U.S. Const. amend. I.
2. John Stuart Mill, *On Liberty*, in *John Stuart Mill: A Selection of His Works*, ed. John M. Robson (Toronto: Macmillan of Canada, 1966), 23.
3. Herodotus *The Histories* 5.78.
4. *Kingsley Books, Inc. v. Brown*, 354 U.S. 436, 447 (1957) (Douglas, J., dissenting).
5. Jedidiah Morse, *Annals of the American Revolution* (Hartford, Conn., 1824), 373.
6. *Roth v. United States*, 354 U.S. 476, 488 (1957).
7. *Board of Education v. Pico*, 457 U.S. 853 (1982).
8. *Tinker v. Des Moines Independent Community School District*, 393 U.S. 503 (1969).
9. *Merriam-Webster's Collegiate Dictionary*, 11th ed., s.v.v. "speech" and "communication."
10. Alexander Meiklejohn, *Political Freedom: The Constitutional Powers of the People* (New York: Oxford University Press, 1965), 119.
11. *Id.* at 75 (emphasis added).
12. *Thornhill v. Alabama*, 310 U.S. 88, 101 (1940).
13. *Schenck v. United States*, 249 U.S. 47, 52 (1919).
14. *Martin v. City of Struthers*, 319 U.S. 141, 143 (1943).
15. *Griswold v. Connecticut*, 381 U.S. 479, 482 (1965) (emphasis added).
16. *Board of Education v. Rowley*, 458 U.S. 176 (1982). See chapter 1 for a discussion of the case.
17. *Serrano v. Priest*, 5 Cal. 3d 584, 608 (1971).
18. *Id.* at 609.
19. *Sweezy v. New Hampshire*, 354 U.S. 234, 250 (1957).
20. *Tinker v. Des Moines Independent Community School District*, 393 U.S. 503, 512 (1969).
21. *Id.* at 506, 512, 513.
22. *Board of Education v. Pico*, 457 U.S. 853, 867 (1982).
23. 20 U.S.C. § 1400(b) (1990).

24. U.S. Department of Education, *To Assure the Free Appropriate Public Education of All Children with Disabilities: Twenty-second Annual Report to Congress on the Implementation of the Individuals with Disabilities Education Act* (Washington, D.C., 2000), A-1.

25. Richard N. Apling, Congressional Research Service, *Individuals with Disabilities Education Act (IDEA): Current Funding Trends*, CRS Report for Congress, no. RL32085 (February 6, 2004).

26. *Thornack v. Boise Independent School District No. 1*, 767 P.2d 1241, 1248 (Idaho 1984).

27. 20 U.S.C. § 1412(a); *see also Board of Education v. Holland*, 786 F. Supp. 874 (E.D. Cal. 1992); *Campbell v. Talladega Board of Education*, 518 F. Supp. 47 (N.D. Ala. 1981).

28. 20 U.S.C. § 1412(a)(5)(A).

29. 34 C.F.R. § 300.324(a)(2)(iv).

30. *Brougham v. Town of Yarmouth*, 823 F. Supp. 9, 15–16 (D. Me. 1993) (emphasis added) (quoting *Board of Education v. Rowley*, 458 U.S. 176, 208 (1982) and *Lachman v. Illinois Board of Education*, 853 F.2d 290, 297 (7th Cir. 1988)).

31. *Petersen v. Hastings Public Schools*, 31 F.3d 705, 708 (8th Cir. 1994).

32. 20 U.S.C. § 1412(a)(5)(A).

5

THE FIRST AMENDMENT AND FREEDOM OF ASSOCIATION

What we have here is a failure to communicate.

—*Cool Hand Luke*

Jean was seven and lived in a city of about 50,000. She attended second grade in a regular classroom in which there were no other deaf or hard of hearing children. She was fluent in ASL—her parents and siblings were also deaf. Although the school had provided her with an interpreter, her interaction with peers was perfunctory, static. She was smart and generally did well in school. Her classmates knew a few signs, but at recess and lunch Jean could usually be found by herself, too often studying the ground or looking into the trees that rimmed the schoolyard. She was eager to attend class and be involved, but she was always on the periphery of things. She had no friends from school and after school went straight home.

One day her parents visited school and arrived during recess. They saw their daughter alone on the playground. She was normally a vibrant child, but standing alone she seemed only sad. Jean's mother cried when she returned home. The next day, her parents wrote the school requesting that Jean go to the state school for the deaf. The state school was three hundred miles away, and Jean would be a residential student. Her parents understood this, knew that their seven-year-old daughter would wake up every morning and go to bed every night in a distant place. But she wouldn't stand by herself on the playground.

After dinner and homework, they asked Jean about moving to the state school. She had been there many times—her brother and sister had attended, as had her parents. She immediately ran upstairs, and when her parents came up to put her to bed, they found a small suitcase packed and placed next to her bedroom door.

The IEP meeting did not go well. The school administrator explained to Jean's parents that the LRE requirement of the law prohibited the district from sending a child to a more restrictive environment if she could attend regular school. The interpreter was the "supplementary aid" that allowed her to "achieve satisfactorily" in the regular classroom. The administrator knew the IDEA regulations well and knew that the federal government would criticize any school district that did not meet the important LRE mandate.

"The state school was very good for me, my wife, and our other children," Jean's father said. "Jean is no different."

The administrator nodded and filled out the rest of the IEP, saying, without looking up, "The school district is offering continued placement in the regular second-grade class, and your request for placement at the state school has been denied."

When Jean's parents told Jean of the school administrator's decision, she cried and asked why she couldn't go to the state school. When they explained that the district would not let her, she stomped upstairs. Her suitcase remained next to the door.

Jean's parents filed for a due process hearing. At the hearing, her parents testified about Jean and her increasing sadness. "She has always been a vibrant, even stubborn, child," her father explained. "But lately she has been spending too much time in her room. She never plays with any other children."

"Have you talked to your pediatrician about Jean's so-called moods?" the school's attorney asked.

"No."

"Is she receiving any therapy?"

"No."

"Has her doctor said that she has any mental illness?"

"No."

"Has her doctor expressed any concern about her developmental growth?"

"No."

"Has her doctor recommended any help for any mental problems?"

"No."

"So she has no mental disturbances as defined by the IDEA?"

"No."*

---

*I represented Jean, and this specific exchange reveals the harsh burden on children like her. The IDEA provides that a child can be "removed" from a regular classroom only if the child is not achieving satisfactorily. 20 U.S.C. § 1412(a)(5). Jean needed to show signs of mental disease to have the right to access a language-appropriate school.

Jean's parents asked a deaf teacher from the state school to testify. He signed, with an interpreter voicing, of his own experiences as the only deaf child in his school district, of his loneliness, of the lack of communication opportunities, of his feelings of being liberated when he went to the state school. He testified about the rich language environment at the state school. He said that he had visited Jean's current class. "It is linguistically arid and empty."

"Do you know about the IDEA's least restrictive environment requirement?" the school's attorney asked.

"Yes," the teacher signed.

"Do you know that Congress disfavored placement in which there are few or no nondisabled children?"

"Deaf children are not disabled but simply communicate differently."

The attorney then read into the record the list of "disability" categories under the IDEA, which included "hearing impairment."

"Do you want to change your answer to the previous question?"

"No."

The parents called an expert from a state assessment center. She had worked with deaf children for more than twenty years and explained that as a deaf child grew older and the language in a classroom grew more complex, the isolation grew and the chances of the child developing appropriate linguistic, psychological, and social skills diminished. The assessor saw incipient signs of unhappiness and even some depression in Jean.

"Have you reviewed the school's assessment of Jean?" the school's attorney asked.

"Yes."

"Please turn to page 8. Is it true that Jean is functioning at grade level, is scoring at the above-average level in reading comprehension, and finally, is showing appropriate emotional development? Indeed, there is no evidence, is there Doctor, that anything is going wrong with Jean?"

The expert explained that by the time trouble appeared, it would be too late. Jean was beginning to show signs of shutting down socially and emotionally.

"Is there any current evidence that Jean has a mood disorder or a depressive or anxiety disorder?"

"No."

The attorney asked whether the school could make a current decision based on something that might or might not happen in the future.

The school district called Jean's teacher, interpreter, and school counselor. All testified that Jean's grades were good, that although she was not the most active student socially, she seemed to relate to other children, and that with the interpreter, Jean had access to the communication and language in the classroom.

"Does Jean have any friends—that is, peers with whom she plays and chats and has a relationship beyond merely saying 'hello'? Jean's attorney asked each of the witnesses. They all answered that Jean had acquaintances but not what you would call "close friends."

"Does the IDEA require that children with disabilities necessarily have friends?" the school's attorney asked the witnesses.

"Of course all children should have friends, but there is no legal requirement and we can't create friendships or associations for Jean."

"Is there anything in the IDEA that requires the IEP to ensure that such children have friends?" the school's attorney asked.

"I am not aware of anything in the law requiring that the IEP promise that a child will have friends or associations in school," one of the school district's witnesses responded.

Jean's attorney paused, ready to ask another question, but looked at Jean's parents and decided not to. He knew that the IDEA did indeed address this issue of friendship, but in a way that would never appeal to Jean's parents. It defined a child as having an "emotional disturbance" if the child was unable to "build or maintain satisfactory interpersonal relationships with peers and teachers."[1] Thus, to more effectively raise the lack of peer interaction under the IDEA and create a reason to remove Jean from the regular classroom, he would have to show that Jean met a legal standard that would label her "emotionally disturbed." What a trade-off for this proud and effective family. The attorney thought of his hearing daughter, who happened to be about Jean's age, and wondered whether he would accept such a deplorable exchange. He asked for a break and explained the dilemma to Jean's parents, who signed strongly and simply, "No!"

On the last day of the hearing, the school's attorney made a brief statement. "Jean's grades are great, she is in the legal LRE, and although her current placement might not be perfect, it is providing, as required by the IDEA, an appropriate education. Absent a showing that Jean is 'emotionally disturbed' under the law, the school district cannot place her in the state school."

Jean's father signed his closing remarks. His comments were brief. "My daughter is deaf. She uses ASL to communicate. My wife and I went to the state school. My daughter is angry at home. My daughter has no friends. My daughter is deaf and wants to go to the state school. She does not have a mental problem, but like all children, she needs friends. She needs children her age who can sign with her. Would you let that happen to your child? This school is very restrictive for a deaf child!"

Three weeks later the hearing officer issued his decision. Although there were some early signs of difficulty for Jean, she was doing well in school, and without clear and current evidence that she was suffering, the law was clear, particularly the LRE mandate.* Jean must remain in her current placement. The lack of serious friends, though troubling, was not legally sufficient to justify placing her in a more restrictive environment. Jean's suitcase stayed near her bedroom door for the remainder of the school year.

Several months later, Jean's father and mother went back to school and asked again that she be allowed to attend the state school. The school district mailed a copy of the hearing officer's decision to the family. Several weeks later, on a cold morning, Jean's father drove to the school district and parked his car. He took a sign out of the car and, for the next three weeks, marched in front of the school. The sign had a picture of Jean's suitcase. Two months later the school district agreed to place Jean in the state school. It had been almost two years since the dispute had started.

Within two weeks of moving to the state school, Jean had become close friends with 3 other girls and acquainted with just about every one of the 120 elementary children in the school. Her teacher wrote her parents that Jean tended to be a little bossy, but was a good student and always seemed to be on the go. Jean reluctantly came home for Thanksgiving only after she was convinced that the state school would be closed and all her friends would be going home too.

*As in Jean's case, a deaf child must prove severe linguistic or psychological difficulties before the law will allow placement in a language- and peer-rich environment like a state school. In *Poolaw v. Bishop*, 67 F.3d 830 (9th Cir. 1995), the court ruled that a deaf boy should finally go to the Arizona State School for the Deaf and Blind because, at the age of eleven, he was only able to use simple gestures as language.

THE FIRST AMENDMENT AND THE RIGHT TO BE WITH PEERS

> The freedom to enter into and carry on certain intimate
> or private relationships is a fundamental element of lib-
> erty protected by the Bill of Rights. . . . The First
> Amendment protects those relationships . . . "with whom
> one shares not only a special community of thoughts,
> experiences, and beliefs but also distinctively personal as-
> pects of one's life."[2]

The right to associate with others, to have contact with those
of one's choosing, is a central component of the First Amendment.
Although most First Amendment cases focus on controversial
rather than standard matters, the associational right under the First
Amendment has particular resonance for deaf and hard of hearing
people because they seek the most basic of daily relational experiences. They seek, as Jean did, the chance to communicate with
peers, to have friends, and to engage socially, which is central to
both the educational and human experience. The IDEA, particularly the LRE provision, is a barrier to the constitutionally protected right of association.

Can we really argue that this associational right and need is
greater among deaf and hard of hearing children than hearing children? At some level, of course not, for I am not arguing that hearing children have less of a need for association. But a hearing child
can walk into virtually any classroom in America and communicate
and associate with others. The relationship between deaf and hard
of hearing children, limited as it is by population statistics, is con-
tingent on creating and protecting the few unique environments in
which they can communicate directly with their peers. The barriers
imposed between many deaf and hard of hearing children and a
true and rich communication environment are evident in the stories of Jean and Amy Rowley.

The nondeaf world is a particularly closed one for many deaf
and hard of hearing people. The reality is that communication

"out there," whether in the market, the ballpark, the subway, or the classroom, is limited. Jean clearly craved interaction with her peers, but because of the communication barrier, she had no opportunity to develop relationships with her classmates. The irony of the IDEA is that the understandable desire to bring children with disabilities into the mainstream is counterproductive and counterintuitive for Jean and many other deaf or hard of hearing children. For purposes of communication and language, and therefore peer interaction, the regular classroom is the most isolating and the most restrictive, even though it is the least restrictive by law. And even when that placement is appropriate—as it was for Amy—the lack of qualified interpreters may severely limit the right of association.*

If communicating with others makes us human and defines our world, then any law, policy, or institution that restrains that association is dubious at best, cruel at worst. It is well established that peer interaction is central to cognitive development, problem solving, and learning in general.[3] Studies of deaf children who are mainstreamed show that many feel "lonely, rejected, and socially isolated" and find themselves "frustrated in their attempts to relate to or interact with their hearing classmates."[4] By high school, hearing students have obtained about half of their education through socialization. They have learned how to relate to others, how to work in groups, and how to use various communication styles. Many deaf and hard of hearing students find themselves in an "artificial" peer environment where they often rely on a third party (an interpreter) for socialization and interaction. They miss out on the informal chatter that is quite central to the daily communication among adolescents and central to the educational experience.[5]

Current educational policy and law violates the First Amend-

*Clearly, deaf and hard of hearing children have a right to attend a regular classroom, and many of them do. But even these situations are complex. See chapter 3 and, in particular, reference to Gina Oliva's *Alone in the Mainstream*.

ment's associational right of deaf and hard of hearing children. Every time an Amy Rowley is denied a qualified interpreter, every time a Jean is denied the right to attend a school in which she will have a sufficient number of peers with whom she can easily and directly communicate, these associational rights are ignored. In analyzing the key court decisions on the First Amendment right to associate, we see more vividly the value of that right and how rarely it has been applied to deaf and hard of hearing children.

JUDICIAL APPLICATION OF THE FIRST AMENDMENT RIGHT TO ASSOCIATION

The U.S. Supreme Court has frequently and emphatically restated the First Amendment right to association with one's peers and community. In 1984, Justice Brennan wrote that "because the Bill of Rights is designed to secure individual liberty, it must afford the formation and preservation of certain kinds of highly personal relationships a substantial measure of sanctuary from unjustified interference by the State."[6] The Court has recognized the legally and constitutionally important fact that "personal bonds have played a critical role in the culture and traditions of the Nation by cultivating and transmitting shared ideals and beliefs," which in turn "foster diversity and act as critical buffers between the individual and the power of the State."[7] We have a Constitution that protects personal relationships—"the constitutional shelter afforded such relationships reflects the realization that individuals draw much of their emotional enrichment from close ties with others" and that the ability to "define one's identity" is "central to any concept of liberty."[8]

The relationship between one's unique identity (and what creates that identity) and the right and need to associate with others of similar identity is, of course, particularly important for deaf and hard of hearing children, who can be significantly cut off from associating with much of the hearing world. Their association with deaf peers goes to the heart of what the Supreme Court recognizes as those "personal bonds" that cultivate and transmit our "shared ideals and beliefs."

During the civil rights movement of the late 1950s, the State of Alabama sought to stop the work of the local NAACP chapter and to oust it from the state. The NAACP had opened a regional office, had "recruited members and solicited contributions within the state," and had given "financial support and furnished legal assistance to Negro students seeking admission to the [segregated] state university." It had also "supported a Negro boycott of the bus lines in Montgomery to compel the seating of passengers without regard to race." An Alabama state court issued an order restraining the NAACP from engaging in any activities within the state and from taking any further steps to qualify to do business in Alabama. When the NAACP moved to have this order dissolved, the state court ordered that the NAACP produce records, including bank statements, leases, deeds, and "records containing the names and addresses of all its Alabama 'members' and 'agents.'"[9] That the Montgomery bus boycott had recently ushered in the civil rights movement in the South was the undercurrent in this case, and it revealed the steps that states would take to prevent challenges to legal segregation.

When the NAACP did not comply with this order, it was fined $100,000. The NAACP appealed these rulings to the U.S. Supreme Court, which ruled that the associational freedom under the First Amendment was so fundamental that Alabama's action violated the Constitution. "It is beyond debate that freedom to engage in association for the advancement of beliefs and ideas is an inseparable aspect of . . . 'liberty' [and] it is immaterial whether the beliefs sought to be advanced by association pertain to political, economic, religious or cultural matters."[10]

There are two significant aspects of this ruling. First, the Court recognized that the basis of association is unlimited; it is "immaterial" why a group gathers. That the Deaf community is a cultural and linguistic minority only strengthens the associational rights recognized by the Supreme Court. Second, the Alabama effort did not, at least directly, impede the right of African Americans in Alabama to associate but rather to do so formally. The difference, of course, in those blatant Jim Crow days was not significant; gathering informally or formally could be deadly. Jean and her peers could not even associate "informally" let alone through a formal organization. She could not do what all of us, including the citizens of Alabama in 1958, could do—stop and chat with a neighbor, friend, or classmate. She had no political agenda; she sought only the daily benefits of association with other human beings.

Current educational law and policy deny—perhaps without malice, but deny nonetheless—the right of deaf and hard of hearing children to associate with each other and their hearing peers. Let me be clear here that the comparison with the plaintiffs in Alabama is not meant to minimize the associational danger inherent in *NAACP v. Alabama*. When denied their associational rights, deaf and hard of hearing children do not of course face physical danger, but they face fundamental and life-affecting isolation, the very thing the First Amendment intended to avoid.

The denial of deaf and hard of hearing children's right to associate is more striking when we look at how our courts have ruled on the associational rights of so-called subversives. Underlying these decisions is a fundamental question: if individuals may gather to discuss things that most of us find offensive or even dangerous, how can it be that deaf and hard of hearing children are denied the right to associate at all in school?

America has long struggled with its core belief in the right of the individual to think as he or she wishes and to talk with others about those thoughts, on the one hand, and its frequent fear that certain thoughts pose a danger, on the other hand. And yet the cherished belief in the right to associate with whomever one wants and to discuss whatever one chooses to discuss—be it communism or fascism, the evils of democratic capitalism, or the so-called threat to the white race—has long been recognized by our courts.

For example, in 1952, in the midst of the McCarthy era, the U.S. Supreme Court ruled that an Oklahoma law that prohibited individuals who were members of "subversive" organizations from working for the state violated the Constitution. The Court reasoned that "it matters not whether association existed innocently or knowingly," for the inhibition of individual freedom stifles democratic expression.[11]

The right to associate includes the right to express "one's attitudes or philosophies" and opinions. This right is consistent with, and is necessary to protect, our further right of assembly.

> The right of peaceable assembly is a right cognate to those of free speech. . . . "The very idea of a government, republican in form, implies a right on the part of its citizens to meet peaceably for consultation in respect to public affairs" [and] the right is one that cannot be denied without violating those fundamental principles of liberty and justice which lie at the base of all [our] civil and political institutions.[12]

This right to associate is constitutionally protected in our schools. In *Widmar v. Vincent,* university students who belonged to an evangelical Christian group were not allowed to meet in university buildings. Although the Court understood that this was no simple "free speech" case, particularly since it involved the equally important constitutional issue of the separation of church and state, the Court nonetheless ruled that the university action violated the First Amendment right to free speech and association. The Court's comments on the right to speak and associate resonate clearly with the issue of a deaf or hard of hearing child's right to associate with peers in school.

> The University has created a forum generally open for use by student groups [and] has assumed an obligation to justify its discriminations and exclusions under appli-

cable constitutional norms. The Constitution forbids a State to enforce certain exclusions from a forum generally open to the public, even if it was not required to create the forum in the first place.[13]

The importance of this associational right is reflected in the need for Americans to "participate in the intellectual give and take of campus debate,"[14] and that is why "students enjoy First Amendment rights of speech and association on the campus."[15]

Nine years later, the Supreme Court ruled that a public school could not deny a group of students the right to meet to read and discuss the Bible.[16] Again we see the Court's recognition that schools cannot provide associational rights to some but not others, even when there is the countervailing possibility that schools may be viewed as endorsing a religion. Jean (and Amy Rowley), of course, did not seek the right to discuss religion or subversive matters but merely to discuss anything.

A public-school classroom contains few, if any, barriers that prevent students from speaking to, and associating with, each other. A student may be asked to be quiet, two students may be asked to refrain from a private discussion during a class activity, but otherwise students are free to exchange information and associate with others in that exchange. The denial of an interpreter for Amy Rowley, the action of the school system in denying Jean the chance to go to a school where she could freely and appropriately communicate and associate with her classmates, erect the very barriers our courts and Constitution abhor.

Every time a school district denies a student a qualified interpreter or denies a transfer to a class for deaf students because of the IDEA (and the LRE requirement), it interferes with a deaf or hard of hearing child's right to associate. Sometimes this violation is due to ignorance, sometimes it is due to a lack of resources, and often it is due to the fact that schools rely on existing laws. But the motive or lack of motive does not matter, because it is the painful consequences of that denial of First Amendment rights that require our attention and the application of our Constitution.

Imagine if a school allowed students to associate with one another anywhere in school for only three minutes each day. Would there be any doubt that the right to free speech and association was fundamentally restricted?

I believe that these denials are so long-standing, and even subtle, that it is quite startling to pause for a moment and see how constitutionally inappropriate they are. Another year passes, another thousand IEPs are written, another thousand deaf and hard of hearing children struggle through school. But we know how vibrant and important and broadly applicable our Constitution is and how it applies to our right to associate with others: "The Court has recognized that the freedom to enter into and carry on certain intimate or private relationships is a fundamental element of liberty protected by the Bill of Rights."[17] The right to associate and assemble "cannot be denied without violating those fundamental principles of liberty and justice which lie at the base of all civil and political institutions."[18] Although the American school system is not consciously trying to deny these associational rights, the IDEA encourages this denial and, in so doing, violates the First Amendment.

NOTES

1. 34 C.F.R. § 300.8(c)(4).

2. *Board of Directors of Rotary International v. Rotary Club of Duarte,* 481 U.S. 537, 545 (1987) (quoting *Roberts v. U.S. Jaycees,* 468 U.S. 609, 619–620 (1984)).

3. Brenda Schick, "How Might Learning through an Educational Interpreter Influence Cognitive Development?" in *Educational Interpreting,* ed. Elizabeth A. Winston (Washington, D.C., Gallaudet University Press, 2002), 79.

4. Marc Marschark, *Raising and Educating a Deaf Child* (New York: Oxford University Press, 1997), 128.

5. Gina Oliva, *Alone in the Mainstream* (Washington, D.C.: Gallaudet University Press, 2004), 82–83.

6. *Roberts v. U.S. Jaycees*, 468 U.S. 609, 618 (1984).

7. *Id.* at 618–619.

8. *Id.* at 619.

9. *NAACP v. Alabama*, 357 U.S. 449, 452–453 (1958).

10. *Id.* at 460.

11. *Wieman v. Updegraff*, 344 U.S.183, 191 (1952).

12. *De Jonge v. Oregon*, 299 U.S. 353, 364 (1937) (quoting *United States v. Cruikshank*, 92 U.S. 542, 552 (1876)).

13. *Widmar v. Vincent*, 454 U.S. 263, 267–268 (1981).

14. *Healy v. James*, 408 U.S. 169, 181 (1972).

15. *Widmar*, 454 U.S. at 268 n.5.

16. *Board of Education v. Mergens*, 496 U.S. 226 (1990).

17. *Board of Directors of Rotary Int'l v. Rotary Club*, 481 U.S. 537, 545 (1987).

18. *De Jonge*, 299 U.S. at 364.

6

THE IMPORTANCE OF THE FIRST AMENDMENT: PROTECTING THE EXTREMES OF SPEECH

Language is a skin; I rub my language against the other. It is as if I had words instead of fingers, or fingers at the tip of my words.

—Roland Barthes, "Talking"

Brian was born deaf and, like Amy Rowley, had a high IQ. He attended the same school in Florida that he would have attended if he were hearing. He was the only deaf child in the program.[1] Unlike Amy Rowley, Brian's school district agreed to provide him with a sign language interpreter; there was just one problem—Brian's interpreter could not hear very well. The interpreter wore hearing aids, and at times she had difficulty hearing everything that was being said in class by the students and the teacher. Hearing aids generally do not discriminate between sounds, amplifying all noise in the environment. When sounds come from behind a person using hearing aids or when there are other classroom or environmental sounds, the ability to hear what is being said may be compromised.[2]

The interpreter used Pidgin Sign English, whereas Brian used Signed English. Signed English is an artificial signing system that combines the individual signs of ASL with the grammatical structure of English. Additional signs are used to show pluralization, verb endings, prefixes, and suffixes. Pidgin Sign English also uses the signs of ASL but with a mixture of ASL and English grammar.[3] Brian's interpreter had little training, and her only other interpreting experience was with children with emotional difficulties.

Brian understood about 50 percent of what the interpreter signed to him. The interpreter would not have met the requirements of the Registry of Interpreters for the Deaf (RID) if they were applied by the school district—though they were not, because there is no legal requirement

77

to hire certified interpreters. The RID requires that interpreters "transmit everything that is said in exactly the same way it was intended," but the qualifications, hiring, and firing of school-based interpreters is absolutely hit or miss. School resources, interpreter availability, and understanding of hearing loss all affect what is or is not provided to deaf children.[4]

Brian's parents, unlike many others, had the energy, resources, and determination to fight, so they requested a due process hearing. That was both the good and the bad news. It was certainly good in that a neutral third party would render a decision, but it was bad because Brian's most fundamental (and First Amendment) need—the ability to express and receive information in school—was a matter to be fought over rather than a service provided without fuss or debate. Under the IDEA, communication is nothing more than an agenda item for the IEP meeting and an advocacy issue to be won or lost at an administrative hearing.

Communication must be debated, justified, and struggled over year after year, but that is how it goes for deaf and hard of hearing children. The due process request for Brian was made in September 1997, but it was not until December, when school was well under way, that the due process hearing officer ruled that the school district had to provide Brian with another educational interpreter, that an interpreter with her own hearing loss simply would not do. By 1998, Brian still did not have a qualified interpreter, and Brian's parents were forced to go to court to enforce the due process decision. Though the court upheld the hearing officer's decision, Brian lost months and months of access to education during this process.

EVEN THOUGH BRIAN and Amy Rowley had no clear right to classroom information, the First Amendment ensures our right to express and receive callous, hurtful, shameful, libelous, licentious, and even dangerous information, or as Woodrow Wilson said, to "advertise" one's foolishness. It protects that which is low in content or high in profanity. It protects the right to sell diet soda and wear a swastika. And it is in the less appealing sides of our characters that we see how far the First Amendment can and must go to protect the free flow of information in American society and, by contrast, how little it applies to protect any kind of flow for deaf and hard of hearing children.

DANGEROUS SPEECH

Since the creation of our Constitution and the Bill of Rights, there has always been a debate about the right to speak one's mind and the responsibility of the government to protect society from harm, whether the harm is of a physical or psychological nature. Whether it was Abraham Lincoln's effort to suspend habeas corpus, Franklin Roosevelt's signature on Executive Order 9066—which sent Japanese Americans to internment camps in California, Nevada, Wyoming, and Utah—Senator McCarthy's red-baiting, or restrictions on the works of James Joyce or D. H. Lawrence, this conflict between individual liberty and societal safety is an old one.

In our post-9/11 world, the debate is more complex and contentious, but the deeply cherished right to speak one's mind regardless of the subject matter remains vibrant and part of our democratic marrow. Speaking of bad things, articulating thought rather than taking action, remains firmly protected by the First Amendment.

It is easy to protect ideas that are compatible with an individual's or a society's core beliefs; it is a bit more difficult, and therefore more impressive, to protect those ideas that are fundamentally in opposition to those beliefs. And our courts have frequently enough confirmed that real freedom of speech, the real free flow of information, welcomes even dangerous, silly, profane, and libelous information.

In 1951, the New Hampshire legislature passed an act that declared subversive organizations unlawful and subversive persons ineligible for state-government employment. Merely advocating subversive matters was against the law.[5] In 1954, the state attorney general called in Paul Sweezy, a college professor who had served during World War II, for questioning regarding subversive activities. Sweezy answered some of the questions, but he refused to answer others, particularly those involving the Progressive Party in New Hampshire and whether his wife, Nancy Sweezy, and others were members. He refused to answer questions about a lecture he gave to approximately a hundred students at the University of New Hampshire, including whether he said that "socialism was inevitable in this country" or espoused the "theory of dialectical materialism." He refused to answer whether he believed in communism, claiming the First Amendment protected him from such inquiries. A local judge ordered him to jail. The Supreme Court of New Hampshire confirmed this ruling, but the U.S. Supreme Court reversed it, criticizing the "inhibiting effect" of the legislation on the "flow of democratic expression" and the "equally grave" impact on individuals like Sweezy.[6]

The Court found the legislation to be an unwarranted invasion in the areas of "academic freedom and political expression—areas in which government should be extremely reticent to tread"—and asserted that our "form of government is built on the premise that every citizen shall have the right to engage in political expression," a right that must be encouraged through and by our educational system.[7]

Even in a time of significant fear about communism, the Supreme Court realized that when the value of protecting the nation against subversive or dangerous doctrine was weighed against the value of our right to freely exchange thought, particularly in our schools, the right to freely exchange ideas prevailed. The importance of a free flow of information outweighed any potential danger. And so language believed to be dangerous by a significant portion of American society, and restricted by elected representatives, is in fact protected, but the entirety of language in a class is unavailable to a deaf or hard of hearing child.

Ernest Mandel was less circumspect than Paul Sweezy. He believed that the U.S. government should be overthrown. A Belgian journalist and self-proclaimed "revolutionary Marxist," Mandel was prohibited from coming to the United States for several speaking engagements because section 212(a)(28)(D) of the Immigration and Nationality Act of 1952 denied a visa to any "aliens" who "advocate the economic, international and governmental doctrines of world communism." Mr. Mandel addressed one of the conferences by telephone, after which he and his six sponsors filed suit claiming the statute was unconstitutional because it restricted the right to "hear [Mandel's] views and engage him in a free and open academic exchange."[8]

The Supreme Court stated that although Mandel "had no constitutional right of entry to this country," the First Amendment clearly protects the right to "hear, speak, and debate with Mandel in person." As the Court explained, the Constitution "protects the right to *receive information and ideas*" as well as suitable "*access* to social, political, aesthetic, moral, and other ideas and experiences."[9]

In rejecting the government's claim that plaintiffs could exchange ideas with Mandel over the telephone, the Court noted the importance of those "particular qualities inherent in sustained, face-to-face debate, discussion and questioning" and recognized that the constitutional right to access information is "nowhere more vital" than in our schools and universities.[10]

If one has the right to face-to-face exchange with an individual deemed, at least by law, to be dangerous to the well-being of the nation, then what of the right of a deaf or hard of hearing child to have face-to-face exchange with a teacher in a classroom and friends on the playground to discuss the minor and major, but infrequently subversive, matters found in school? The student who is denied the right to receive information from a revolutionary Marxist is denied much; the student who cannot access any information—whether it is the time of that night's basketball game or a debate about whether the government has a duty to keep dangerous individuals out of the country—is denied everything.

The country's future "depends upon leaders trained through wide exposure to that robust exchange of ideas which discovers truth 'out of a multitude of tongues.'"[11] Deaf and hard of hearing children are a vital part of that multitude. This is not to say that speech cannot be limited. We have noted the old saw of "shouting fire in a crowded theater." But the assumption is that speech is limited only in the most unusual and necessary situations. That the Nazi or white supremacist or misogynist may have his or her say stands in stark contrast to a situation in which a deaf or hard of hearing child, without communication access, is denied any flow of information. Is there a difference between a law or policy that actively restricts or prohibits the free expression (and therefore receipt) of ideas, as in the cases involving Sweezy and Mandel, and the IDEA, which has an indirect impact on that expression and receipt? That the IDEA does not directly prohibit the access of deaf and hard of hearing children to the free flow of thought is not palliative. A prohibitory law and one that indirectly has the same impact erect the same unconstitutional barrier.

THE RIGHT TO ANNOY

The First Amendment protects the right of one individual to bother, annoy, or even offend another. Our daily lives are filled with intrusions that are protected because under the shield of liberty, "many types of life, character, opinion and belief can develop unmolested and unobstructed."[12] In this way, the First Amendment runs up against our desire to be left alone, to be free of the opinions or beliefs of others. How do we weigh the right of that fellow over there to speak to us or wave his arms in front of us to get our attention? What of the panhandler who wants us to "help out" or the true believer who seeks to share the joy religion gives him or her? Certainly there are times when such behaviors cross a line and belief becomes assault, but in a democracy there is a good deal we must put up with to ensure that we may all have our say.

For many years Jehovah's Witnesses went door-to-door in a predominately Catholic Connecticut neighborhood. They often left a phonograph record entitled *Enemies,* which included an attack on the Catholic religion. The Jehovah's Witnesses also stopped individuals in the street and asked if they could play the record for them. The Witnesses were charged with and convicted of breaching the peace. In reversing their convictions, the U.S. Supreme Court asserted that

> in the realm of religious faith, and in that of political belief, sharp differences arise. In both fields the tenets of one man may seem the rankest error to his neighbor. To persuade others to his own point of view, the pleader, as we know, at times, resorts to exaggeration, to vilification of men . . . and even to false statement. But the people of this nation have ordained in the light of history, that, in spite of the probability of excesses and abuses, these liberties are, in the long view, essential to an enlightened opinion and right conduct on the part of the citizens of a democracy.[13]

If there is a constitutional right to annoy and intrude, to be excessive in our speech and communication, then how do we tell Amy Rowley or Brian that they have little or no right to be both enlightened and annoyed?

DAMAGING OR LIBELOUS INFORMATION

The right to say dangerous or libelous things is equally protected by our Constitution. In perhaps the most famous libel case, the Supreme Court ruled in *New York Times Co. v. Sullivan* that even though the nationally renowned newspaper had published an advertisement that contained untruths about Sullivan, the First Amendment protected false communications. Sullivan was the commissioner of public affairs who supervised the police department for the city of Montgomery, Alabama. In May 1960, the

Times published a full-page advertisement referring to a "wave of terror by those who would deny" Southern blacks the right to engage in nonviolent demonstrations against racist policies and laws. The ad referred to the police "ringing" the Alabama State College campus and keeping the students "padlocked" inside the dining hall in an "attempt to starve them into submission" and to "Southern violators" bombing Martin Luther King Jr.'s home, almost killing his wife and child.[14] Although some of the facts in this ad were true—police were sent to the college—the police did not ring the campus and did not padlock students inside any buildings. Moreover, the bombing of Dr. King's house occurred before Sullivan became commissioner. When Sullivan contacted the *New York Times,* the paper refused to print a retraction.

At trial, the jury found that the statements regarding Sullivan were libelous by law, malicious, and false and that they caused "legal injury" to Sullivan, who was entitled to general and punitive damages.* In upholding the trial court's decision, the Alabama Supreme Court asserted that words could "injure" a person in his "reputation, profession, trade or business" and could bring him into "public contempt," and therefore ruled that the First Amendment did not protect such "libelous publications."[15] The U.S. Supreme Court overturned the Alabama Supreme Court, holding that a public official could indeed sue for damages when the statement was false and made with "reckless disregard of whether it was false or not," but that nonreckless *falsehoods* were part of the spirited and open debate about our government.[16] "[The] erroneous statement is inevitable in free debate," the Court wrote. "The constitutional protection does not turn upon the 'truth, popularity, or social utility of the ideas and beliefs which are offered.'"[17]

---

*In a civil lawsuit, punitive damages can be awarded for behavior that is so wrong and extreme as to justify "punishment" to the defendant in the form of an additional money award. The plaintiffs in the *New York Times* case sought $5,600,000 in damages from the newspaper.

The millions of readers of the *New York Times* had no barriers placed before them to read clearly false statements; Brian and Amy could access neither true nor false information in their classrooms.

HATEFUL COMMUNICATION

This right to express and receive negative information includes the right to say (and do) hateful things. The First Amendment recognizes that to try to distinguish good and bad communication, to allow that which is kind but not that which is hateful or cruel, not only is a difficult proposition but creates First Amendment distinctions that inherently weaken the right. The value of a free flow of information may be no more starkly drawn and is best understood when one burns a cross as an expression of blatant racism and seeks and is provided the protection of the First Amendment.

In 1990, several St. Paul, Minnesota, teenagers burned a cross in the yard of an African American family that lived in their neighborhood. The St. Paul Bias-Motivated Crime Ordinance provided that

> whoever places on public or private property a symbol, object, appellation, characterization or graffiti, including, but not limited to, a burning cross or Nazi swastika, which one knows or has reasonable grounds to know arouses anger, alarm or resentment in others on the basis of race, color, creed, religion or gender, commits disorderly conduct and shall be guilty of a misdemeanor.[18]

Even though freedom of speech and communication is not absolute, because there are some areas of "speech" in which its "slight social value as a step to truth" is "clearly outweighed by the social interest in order and morality," the U.S. Supreme Court still found the ordinance unconstitutional because it limited speech based solely on the subject of the speech.[19]*

In finding the ordinance unconstitutional, the Court noted the differences between the act of expression and the expression itself: burning a flag may violate an ordinance against outdoor fires, but the statement made is protected. The Court concluded that even something as abhorrent as cross burning was protected by the First Amendment. It would not sanction "selective limitations on speech," even though the Court believed "that burning a cross in someone's front yard is reprehensible. But St. Paul has sufficient means at its disposal to prevent such behavior without adding the First Amendment to the fire."[20]

The free flow of communication will inevitably run up against legitimate concerns about the content and impact of the communication, and there will be times when social order justifies stopping or limiting that flow. But as a general rule, our Constitution frowns upon limitations of the free flow of information, for, as Judge Learned Hand said, "the right conclusions are more likely to be gathered out of a multitude of tongues."[21]

COMMERCIAL INFORMATION

When we think of the right to express and receive information, we think of grand notions, of debates about politics and values, but the First Amendment is not generally interested in the quality or depth of the information. And so although Amy Rowley was not

*Congress can restrict speech of course, can set limits on the content of what we express and receive. There is no blanket protection for pornography or defamation; much depends on what is said and even "where" it is said. Pornography can be accessed in some places but not in schools. Had the *New York Times* been "malicious" in its ad, Sullivan might have won his case. There are "categories of speech entirely invisible to the Constitution, so that they may be made the vehicles for content discrimination." *R.A.V. v. City of St. Paul,* 505 U.S. 377, 383–384 (1992).

entitled to access information circulating in her class, the First Amendment protects our right to express and receive information about diet sodas and video games.

In the 1970s, Virginia law banned the advertising of prescription drug prices. The Supreme Court ruled that the law was unconstitutional and that commercial speech was protected by the First Amendment. The fact that speech involved a commercial transaction did not remove it from the "exposition of ideas" and from the "truth, science, morality, and arts" and thus did not place it beyond constitutional protection.[22] Advertising, "however tasteless and excessive it sometimes may seem, is nonetheless dissemination of information as to who is producing and selling what product, for what reason and for what price."[23] To argue whether a particular expression—whether political or commercial—carries a greater or lesser constitutional imprimatur is, as the Court stressed, "highly paternalistic" because "people will perceive their own best interests if only they are well enough informed, and . . . the best means to that end is to *open the channels of communication* rather than close them."[24]

Allow individuals to receive and express information, and they will decide what is best for them, what they may want to consider or ignore. Open the channels of communication, and the First Amendment is effectively and positively served. And if the free flow of information—including ads to persuade us to buy something, anything—is "indispensable" to an "intelligent and well-informed" populace, then providing full access to information in our educational institutions is a triple value by comparison. If the First Amendment protects the right to sell diet sodas, a child's right to communication must be worthy of comparable safeguarding.

Although the First Amendment promotes public decision making in our democracy, for too long deaf and hard of hearing children have experienced a restricted flow of information, often because of interpreters who cannot effectively interpret, teachers who cannot communicate with their students, and a lack of access to those environments in which that flow of information is direct and open. The U.S. Supreme Court's ruling in *Virginia Pharmacy Board* is particularly relevant here: "We are aware of no general principle that freedom of speech may be abridged when the speaker's listeners could come by his message by some other means."[25]

If there is some value to providing information about medications, consider the applicability of the First Amendment to a product described by the Supreme Court as "perhaps the single most significant threat to public health in the United States"—cigarettes.[26] In 1999, Massachusetts issued regulations to eliminate deception in the marketing, selling, and distribution of cigarettes and smokeless tobacco to children. Among other things, the regulations prevented (1) outdoor advertising in any stadium or retail establishment within a 1,000-foot radius of any public playground or elementary or secondary school and (2) any "point of sale" advertising placed lower than five feet from the floor of any retail business located within a 1,000-foot radius of a school or playground.[27]

The tobacco industry had contended that the ban meant that between 87 and 91 percent of Boston, Worcester, and Springfield would be off-limits to tobacco advertising. The State of Massachusetts disputed those numbers but did admit that the reach would be substantial. To the Court, the regulations meant a nearly "complete ban on the communication of truthful information about smokeless tobacco and cigars to adult consumers, and it ruled that the regulations were excessively broad and violated the First Amendment."[28]*

*It is natural to want to judge products (and their ads) and apply the First Amendment according to a sense of fairness or decency or even concern. After all, as the Court noted in the Massachusetts case, the National Cancer Institute had found that there was a serious increase in the use of tobacco, including smokeless tobacco among children. Why should the First Amendment protect such products and their inducements? In fact,

Although the Court recognized that Massachusetts could restrict speech, the justices stressed that a speech regulation "cannot unduly impinge on the speaker's ability to propose a commercial transaction and the adult listener's *opportunity to obtain information about products.*"[29] Such language hardly suggests the exchange of meaningful intellectual transactions between writer and reader or orator and audience, yet in its practicality we see that the Court does not want to get into the business of distinguishing among the types of communication humans express and receive. In the *Rowley* case, the Supreme Court saw no First Amendment issues for Amy,[30] but in the Massachusetts case it ruled that the "tobacco industry has a *protected interest* in communicating information about its products and adult customers have an interest in *receiving that information.*"[31]

The *Rowley* decision remains mystifying in light of a decision regarding attorney advertising. In that case, the Court noted that

> the listener's interest is substantial: the consumer's concern for free flow of commercial speech often may be far keener than his concern for urgent political dialogue. Moreover, significant societal interests are served by such speech. Advertising, though entirely commercial, may often carry information of import to significant issues of the day. . . . Commercial speech serves to inform the public of the availability, nature, and prices of products and services, and thus performs an indispensable role in the allocation of resources in a free enterprise system.[32]

OBSCENITY

The ultimate value of the First Amendment may be ironically and best reflected in the Supreme Court's rulings on obscenity. As with

the First Amendment does not provide a constitutional haven for advertising cigarettes to children, but it does protect the rights of adults to read about a product that is demonstrably as dangerous for children as adults.

all speech, the burden is on the government to justify the restriction, and indeed, a good deal of obscene material falls well within the reach of the First Amendment's "free flow of information" standard.

In 1983, *Hustler* magazine ran a parody of an advertisement for Campari Liqueur in which Jerry Falwell spoke of his "first time," part of a series of ads in which celebrities talked about their first sexual experience. In the *Hustler* spoof, Mr. Falwell's "first time" was with his mother during a drunken spree in an outhouse. *Hustler* did note that the ad was a parody and "not to be taken seriously."[33] Jerry Falwell sued *Hustler* for libel, invasion of privacy, and intentional infliction of emotional distress. The trial court ruled in favor of *Hustler* regarding the invasion-of-privacy and libel claims but awarded Falwell $150,000 in damages for the infliction of emotional distress. The appeals court affirmed these decisions, but the Supreme Court reversed the award of damages because *Hustler* and its owner Larry Flynt were protected by the First Amendment.

Although it was clear that the *Hustler* ad might be construed as "sufficiently outrageous" as to take it outside the protection of the First Amendment, the Supreme Court would not go that far. The Court focused on the need for a lively and unrestricted public exchange of information regarding public figures like Jerry Falwell. The Court found the *Hustler* caricature of Falwell and his mother "at best a distant cousin of . . . political cartoons . . . and a rather poor relation at that," but still there is no clear and applicable standard of "outrageousness" that would allow the First Amendment to choose between appropriate and inappropriate speech. As the Court ruled, it is expression of opinion that is offensive that may require the greatest constitutional protection, for it is a "central tenet of the First Amendment that the government must remain neutral in the marketplace of ideas."[34]*

That something may be dangerous does not mean that it lacks First Amendment protection.

*The Supreme Court ruled unconstitutional a Georgia law that lead to the arrest of a man who was viewing an 8-millimeter adult film in his own bedroom, noting that "it is well established that the Constitution protects

The irony then is that the First Amendment protects—as it should—the flow of hateful, libelous, annoying, dangerous, commercial, and obscene information but does not protect the rights of deaf and hard of hearing students to receive and express educational information. If our Constitution protects the cigarette industry and Hustler magazine, it certainly must protect Amy Rowley and others like her.

NOTES

1. *In re Ascension Parish School Board*, 27 I.D.E.L.R. (LRP) 646 ([court/jurisdiction] 1997).
2. *See, e.g.*, Marc Marschark, ed., *Raising and Educating a Deaf Child* (New York: Oxford University Press, 1997), 37–38.
3. See *id.* at 50–64 for a discussion of sign language and signing systems.
4. *In re Ascension Parish School Board*, 27 I.D.E.L.R. at 654–655.
5. N.H. Rev. Stat. Ann. § 588:2 (1955) (repealed 1973).
6. *Sweezy v. New Hampshire*, 354 U.S. 234, 250 (1957).
7. *Id.*
8. *Kleindienst v. Mandel*, 408 U.S. 753, 760, 762 (1972).
9. *Id.* at 763 (emphasis added).
10. *Id.* at 763, 765.
11. *Keyishian v. Board of Regents of the University of the State of New York*, 385 U.S. 589, 603 (1967) (quoting *United States v. Associated Press*, 52 F. Supp. 362, 372 (S.D.N.Y. 1943)).
12. *Cantwell v. Connecticut*, 310 U.S. 296, 310 (1940).
13. *Id.*
14. *New York Times Co. v. Sullivan*, 376 U.S. 254, 257 (1964).
15. *Id.* at 254, 263.
16. *Id.* at 280.
17. *Id.* at 271 (quoting *NAACP v. Button*, 371 U.S. 415, 445 (1963)).
18. *R.A.V. v. City of St. Paul*, 505 U.S. 377, 380 (1992).
19. *Id.* at 383 (quoting *Chaplinsky v. New Hampshire*, 315 U.S. 568, 572 (1942)).

the right to receive information and ideas." *Stanley v. Georgia*, 394 U.S. 557, 564 (1969).

20. *Id.* at 396.

21. *United States v. Associated Press*, 52 F. Supp. 362, 372 (S.D.N.Y. 1943).

22. *Virginia Pharmacy Board v. Virginia Consumer Council*, 425 U.S. 748, 762 (1976) (quoting *Chaplinsky v. New Hampshire*, 315 U.S. 568, 572 (1942) and *Roth v. United States*, 354 U.S. 476, 484 (1957)).

23. *Id. at* 765.

24. *Id.* at 770 (emphasis added).

25. *Id.* at 757 n.15.

26. *FDA v. Brown & Williamson*, 529 U.S.120, 161 (2000).

27. *Lorillard Tobacco Co. v. Reilly*, 533 U.S. 525, 534–536 (2001).

28. *Id.* at 564.

29. *Id.* at 565 (emphasis added).

30. *Board of Education v. Rowley*, 458 U.S. 176 (1982). See chapter 1 for a discussion of the case and the Court's ruling.

31. *Lorillard Tobacco*, 533 U.S. at 571 (emphasis added).

32. *Bates v. State Bar of Arizona*, 433 U.S. 350, 364 (1977).

33. *Hustler Magazine, Inc. v. Falwell*, 485 U.S. 46, 48 (1988).

34. *Id.* at 55.

7

INTRODUCTION TO THE
FOURTEENTH AMENDMENT

*No State shall make or enforce any law which shall abridge
the privileges or immunities of citizens of the United States;
nor shall any State deprive any person of life, liberty, or
property, without due process of law; nor deny to any person
within its jurisdiction the equal protection of the laws.*

—U.S. Constitution, Amendment XIV, Section 1

The bell rang, and the teacher stood up and went to the black-board.

"Good morning class. I'm Mr. Howell, and welcome to the first day of school. I hope you all had a good summer, are well rested, and are eager. We have a lot to learn this year, and I know we are going to work hard."

After a couple of questions about lunchtime, the students took out a math workbook. As they began several problems, a new student walked into the class, accompanied by the school principal. The student stood by the wall as the principal spoke briefly to Mr. Howell. After the principal left, the teacher asked for the class's attention.

"Class, this is Philip. He just moved here. He can't hear very well, but I know you'll help him out. Philip, take a seat in the back."

Philip looked intently at Mr. Howell but did not move.

"Philip. That is fine. Just sit over there. See the empty seat to your right?" He pronounced each word with great emphasis. He pointed to an empty seat.

At recess, several students came up to Philip and asked about his hearing aid. Several pointed and laughed.

On the second day, Philip stayed after school. He asked Mr. Howell if he could sit in the front row. Mr. Howell did not look up from his paperwork. "Philip, I have a seating chart, and students are seated alphabetically. Since your last name begins with an *R*, your seat is toward the back."

"But in my other school I could always sit in the first row."

"What did you say?"

Philip repeated his statement. "Well, Philip, you're not in the other school." After one day, Mr. Howell was losing patience with having to repeat himself and speak more slowly. No one at the school asked whether he wanted a deaf child, and they were not giving him any support for Philip.

Several weeks into the school year, Philip's parents met with the principal. They brought a list of concerns and read them to the principal. Philip was working very hard to improve his ability to lipread and to pronounce words. If he sat in the back of the class, it was almost impossible to understand what Mr. Howell was saying. Second, almost every day when the class was doing individual work at their desks, Philip would concentrate very hard on the workbook or the social studies reading assignment, and when Mr. Howell got the class's attention, Philip would continue to work. Once, Mr. Howell threw an eraser at Philip to get his attention. Several times Mr. Howell would ask Philip, "Can you hear me now? Philip?" The other kids would laugh. Another time, Philip was giving a class report and kept using the *w* sound for a word that begin with *r*. Mr. Howell corrected Philip, but Philip continued to use the *w* sound. Mr. Howell threw up his arms and asked Philip to stop his report.

Mr. Howell did not seem to be aware that when he gave a lecture, he tended to walk around the class, which meant that his back was frequently turned to Philip, making it impossible for Philip to try to lip-read what Mr. Howell was saying. He often spoke and wrote on the blackboard at the same time, creating a similar problem for Philip.

At other times, Mr. Howell would show movies or even use something that had been tape-recorded. It was very difficult for Philip to understand these school activities. When Philip's parents asked Mr. Howell to try to accommodate Philip's needs and to move him to the front row, Mr. Howell said that he was sorry but that Philip would have to get used to the real world—that was the way it would be for people who are "deaf and dumb."

The principal expressed her regret about this and asked if they had any suggestions. They wondered whether it would take the burden off Mr. Howell if Philip had a note taker or an interpreter. They also asked if Philip might have speech therapy. The principal said that she would talk to Mr. Howell about changing his seating policy, but could not promise anything. "Mr. Howell has been teaching for a long time and is very set in his ways. As to the note taker or interpreter, our special-education budget is way over, and I can't possibly take money out of the regular education budget just for one student. You wouldn't want the other children to lose something in their education because of Philip, would you?"

THE BROAD CONCEPT OF "EQUAL EDUCATION" AND A WEIGHING OF DIFFICULTIES

AT THE HEART of our constitutional system is the principle that all Americans should be treated the same under our laws. This right to the "equal protection" of the law has a clear logic—the law is blind, and the rules should be the same for all. If white children are allowed to attend a public school, nonwhite children must also be given that right. If all men are allowed to vote, then all women must be allowed to vote. If all those over a certain age can secure a driver's license, that right cannot be denied to Chinese Americans or individuals who did not graduate from high school.

If most students are entitled to try out for the high school baseball team, then the opportunity to try out can't be denied to the other students. Can there be a right more firmly planted in every individual's sense that he or she is entitled to the same opportunity (if not the same results) as others? It goes against our nature to be told that we cannot try to do something that everyone else is trying to do. We may not make the team, we may not pass the driving test, we may not fully grasp the teacher's lecture, but we have the right, under our Constitution, to give it a go and to succeed or fail. Deaf and hard of hearing children have a right to access and develop communication and language in school, and the failure to provide both is a violation of the constitutional right to be treated equally under the Fourteenth Amendment to the U.S. Constitution.*

The most famous equal protection case—*Brown v. Board of Education*—ended the legal segregation of the races in education, not only because educational resources were significantly dissimilar in white and African American schools but because the emotional and cognitive impact of segregation on the child was powerful. The evidence that "separate but equal" was separate but certainly not equal was reflected in a mountain of statistics and anecdotal information regarding school budgets. For example, in 1932, South Carolina spent $331,000 on bus transportation for white students and $628 on transportation for African American students. Only eighty-seven African American students in all of South Carolina had transportation to school.[1] This was inequality and a failure of equal protection at its most profound.

It is futile to try to compare historic woes. What is more vile, racism or anti-Semitism? Are the vestiges of sexism worse than those of homophobia? Certainly, there is little to compare with the institution of slavery in America and its Jim Crow aftermath, de facto segregation, and the ongoing blatant and subtle racism in America. By referring to these issues in the context of a deaf or hard of hearing child's right to equal protection, there is no intent to minimize or marginalize that history or its impact. Yet deaf and hard of hearing children have been denied the equal protection of the law under the IDEA.

When a deaf or hard of hearing child cannot understand what the teacher is lecturing about in class or cannot take certain classes because there is no qualified interpreter, that child is being denied the equal protection of our laws. When another child is not provided instruction to develop age-appropriate language skills or is

*That creating "access" may involve resources is a different, but important, issue. Providing children in wheelchairs with ramps to access schoolrooms involves both a cost and a right. Providing all hearing children with a reading program involves both a cost and a right.

prevented from attending a school in which he or she can communicate directly with his or her peers, the Constitution is not being equally applied. When Amy Rowley was denied access to most of the communication in her classroom that was readily available to her classmates, she was not being treated equally as required by the Fourteenth Amendment to the U.S. Constitution. When Joey (discussed in chapter 3) was provided with an interpreter who knew only those signs Joey taught her, Joey was denied equal protection of the law. Although deaf and hard of hearing students are not denied entrance to public schools as African American children were, the lack of support and funding for linguistic services and placement creates a powerful barrier to their education. Providing an interpreter who cannot sign bars a deaf child from an equal education in ways not dissimilar to the way African American children were barred from an equal education in the pre-*Brown* days.

The Constitution protects all Americans. It is not acceptable that deaf and hard of hearing children are denied the most basic components of an education in our democracy, a right that "must be made available to all on equal terms."[2]

EQUAL PROTECTION: AN OVERVIEW OF DIFFERENT FOURTEENTH AMENDMENT TESTS

The equal protection clause of the Fourteenth Amendment has, perhaps more than any other constitutional requirement, changed and challenged our nation. The clause does not apply to all aspects of American society; it is specifically intended to cover those laws, policies, programs, and other activities of government, not generally private activity.* Equal protection is a profound and powerful

---

*Discrimination in the private sector is covered through legislation; for example, Title VII of the Civil Rights Act of 1964, Pub. L. No. 88-352, 78 Stat. 241 (codified as amended at 42 U.S.C. §§ 2000e *et seq.*), makes it illegal to discriminate in employment based on race, gender, color, religion, or national origin.

concept, but it does not mean that all people have all rights all the time. Our laws, policies, and programs do distinguish between one person and another, one group and another.

The law says that a sixteen-year-old has the right to try to secure a driver's license, but not so a ten-year-old. In some states a felon cannot vote, whereas someone convicted of a misdemeanor can. Students with a certain grade point average and SAT score will be accepted into a state university; those with lower grades and SAT scores will not. I cannot force the FAA to give me a pilot's license to fly a jet just because the equal protection clause of the Fourteenth Amendment says all citizens must be treated the same.

There is common sense to all of this—my claim to a pilot's license merely because I want it is obviously silly; a ten-year-old should not drive a car. An individual who did not graduate from high school cannot claim an equal protection violation when a state university denies him or her entrance. On the other hand, if that university denies entrance to an otherwise qualified applicant who happens to be a woman or African American or gay or Chinese American, very serious equal protection issues are evident— just as evident as when policies or laws deny a deaf child access to 50 percent of classroom communication or deny a child the right to attend the only school in which there are other children with whom to communicate or do not allow a hard of hearing child to sit in the front row of the classroom.

Over the years, our courts have clarified the meaning of the Fourteenth Amendment and when it applies. Tests have been established that help us determine when a violation of equal protection has occurred. Any governmental action that distinguishes one person from another on the basis of race, nationality, or color (the "suspect classes") or affects a fundamental right—the right to assemble, the right to free speech—will be the hardest to justify in light of the Fourteenth Amendment. The state must prove that there is a "compelling" state purpose served by the distinction, and its action will be subject to the strict scrutiny of the reviewing court. It is presumed that such governmental action violates the Fourteenth Amendment, and the government has a very heavy burden to prove otherwise. In short, any policy, program, law, or action that treats a suspect class differently or affects a fundamental right has the greatest chance of running afoul of the Fourteenth Amendment and therefore being unconstitutional.

Of course, the moment in history has much to do with the application of this equal protection right. For example, in times of war, the burden may be reduced so that the government can justify unequal treatment of people or can limit civil liberties. Franklin Roosevelt approved the internment of Japanese Americans during World War II, and the courts ruled that the unequal treatment was justified. That those concerns do not hold up well to the test of time does not alter the fact that equal protection was not applied then by our courts.*

Suspect classes are defined by the *immutable* or unchangeable characteristics of their members. One is struck almost immediately by the immutability or unchangeability of a hearing loss. A hearing loss can be mitigated through hearing aids or cochlear implants, but it cannot be cured. It is a condition that is fundamentally unchangeable or "immutable." If we take our laws, the Constitution, and Supreme Court decisions at their word, deaf and hard of hearing children (and adults) have a case to make that they should

*President Roosevelt's issuance of Executive Order No. 9066 withstood constitutional scrutiny because, at the time at least, the sense (if not the reality) of an internal Japanese threat was very strong. For Roosevelt and no doubt many Americans, the different treatment of Japanese Americans was justified because the perceived "threat" was greater than the loss of freedom. The U.S. Supreme Court upheld Executive Order No. 9066 in several cases, noting in one that although the "distinctions between citizens solely because of their ancestry are by their very nature odious to a free people" and thus "legislative classification or discrimination based on race alone has often been held to be a denial of equal protection," the exigencies of war outweighed that concern. *Hirabayashi v. United States,* 320 U.S. 81, 100 (1943).

be considered a suspect class for purposes of applying the Fourteenth Amendment when analyzing laws and policies that affect them.

The constitutionality of governmental action that distinguishes on the basis of something other than race—for example, gender, age, wealth, or disability—depends on whether there is a "rational basis" for the particular law or action, whether a legitimate governmental purpose is served by the distinction. That is why a ten-year-old who challenges the minimum-age driving law will lose. The legislative determination makes sense, relates to a justifiable state interest, and is therefore "rational" and constitutionally sound. (Any parent, of course, will tell you it would be quite rational if the state passed a law making it illegal for anyone under twenty-five to drive.) But there are many distinctions that are much harder to assess. Not allowing gay people to marry reflects the cultural and religious values of many Americans, but whether that justifies allowing me but not my gay neighbor to marry is fundamentally less clear than the conclusion that denying the car keys to the ten-year-old is justified on safety grounds.

There are, of course, some loopholes in the standard. For example, gender would seem an immutable characteristic, and in fact, the courts have struggled with this apparent inconsistency and created an intermediate test for gender-based discrimination. The standard in these cases is not as strict as that applied to suspect-class matters but is more burdensome than the rational-basis test. Distinctions based on illegitimacy, alien status, wealth, and language sometimes are viewed with greater skepticism than those exclusively in the rational-basis arena. But generally the burden on the government in "rational basis" cases is less difficult to meet, and unlike in "suspect class" cases, the presumption is that the "distinction" is justified.

Certainly the Fourteenth Amendment test that applies to deaf and hard of hearing children—strict scrutiny or rational basis—has important implications; even if the easier standard applies, we must ask whether hiring an interpreter who cannot hear or denying a deaf child access to classroom communication can ever be rational. I would argue that regardless of the standard applied, the failures described here represent significant and clear-cut violations of the equal protection clause of the Fourteenth Amendment.

THE RIGHT TO AN EDUCATION UNDER THE FOURTEENTH AMENDMENT

Education has a particularly unique status in American society. It is the central institution of our democracy, and it carries and conveys our intellectual, economic, artistic, technical, social, linguistic, and creative hopes.[3] No other institution has so direct an impact on that which is closest to our hearts—our children. What other aspect of our lives is compulsory by government determination? We are not required to drive, vote, work, buy property, marry, or pray, but we are required to go to school.* That educational policies, programs, and laws distinguish between deaf and hard of hearing children and hearing children within a compulsory system heightens the equal protection nature of that discrimination and undermines the rationale for the distinctions. If you are going to

---

*When the plaintiffs in *Brown v. Board of Education* asked the U.S. Supreme Court to declare that segregated education violated the Fourteenth Amendment to the Constitution, the Court specifically asked the attorneys in the case to research and report to the Court whether Congress in 1866 meant for the Fourteenth Amendment to apply to segregated education. The best lawyers and historians on both sides of the case found little in the congressional debates of 1866 about the issue—education in 1866 was simply not a very important American concern and certainly was not required. By 2000, education was compulsory in every state, and we spent $357,955,487,000 on elementary and secondary education in America. Andrew T. LeFevre, *Report Card on American Education: A State by State Analysis, 1981–2003* (Washington, D.C.: American Legislative Executive Council, 2004), 62, also available online at http://www.alec.org/meSWFiles/pdf/2004_Report_Card_on_Education.pdf.

require something of citizens but at the same time deny them the right to access the very thing they must attend by law, it is hard to see any "rational" basis for the IDEA and its prohibitive impact on deaf and hard of hearing students.

What does education encompass, and what should be available to all children? Legislatures and local school boards set the curriculum and broad educational goals. They determine what children should and should not learn, which books students can read, whether a teacher can mention intelligent design in the context of teaching evolution, and whether students must demonstrate quantifiable proof that they understand algebraic formulas in order to graduate from high school. Public education involves the development of basic skills in reading, writing, and mathematics, and the teaching of subject matter deemed essential for children and society.

It is in the provision of a wide-ranging education—from physiology to Latin to auto shop to weekly high school newspapers to water polo teams to chess and debate clubs to dances and rallies to punishment for bad behavior—that the real foundation of education becomes evident: it is the ongoing, rich, and necessary exchange of ideas, the free flow of information, our right to know. In the chapters on the First Amendment, I discussed the right to receive and express ideas and information; here, through the perspective of the Fourteenth Amendment, we see that once you provide that "flow"—however broad or limited it may be in any one school system—it must be provided to all.

The Fourteenth Amendment also requires that if a curriculum is mandated, and with it the necessary staff, material, and classes to teach that curriculum, then the resources and processes necessary to ensure that all students have access to that curriculum must be provided. If certain basic skills are taught in school, both for their own importance and as a base on which to build other skills, then the Fourteenth Amendment requires that those skills be taught to all students. If reading and language skills are taught to ensure that students are literate and therefore able to develop more sophisticated skills, then providing deaf and hard of hearing children with language development in school is necessary to ensure that they have the same opportunity to develop literacy and academic skills.

This is so unless there is a justification for adopting a different set of rules for deaf and hard of hearing children. And it is difficult to think that such a distinction is either just or rational.

BROWN AND THE RIGHT TO AN EQUAL EDUCATION

The story of *Brown v. Board of Education* is as close to a mythic American tale as any. The case applies (or should apply) to deaf and hard of hearing children because the Supreme Court established the legal rule that once the state provides education, it must do so for all and equally. In *Brown*, the U.S. Supreme Court overturned *Plessy v. Ferguson*, an 1896 Supreme Court decision upholding racial segregation.[4]

To read the details of the *Brown* litigation and the decades of work that preceded it—the miles covered and tiny Southern rural courts visited by Thurgood Marshall, Oliver Hill, Spottswood Robinson, and others; the homes, jobs, and lives lost to the effort—is to fully appreciate its magnitude. The true value of *Brown* has been debated many times, but there can be no uncertainty that a law that told a child she could not enter the doors of a public school because of her race is abhorrent to our Constitution and national values.

The case involved "separate but equal" schools in Kansas, Virginia, South Carolina, Delaware, and the District of Columbia and an army of attorneys on both sides, including a future Supreme Court justice (Marshall) and a former Democratic presidential nominee (John W. Davies). The future chief justice William H.

Rehnquist was Justice Jackson's law clerk and argued (unsuccessfully) to Jackson that *Plessy* "was right and should be reaffirmed."[5]

The Court held two separate oral arguments; thousands of pages of briefs and exhibits were compiled, submitted, and reviewed; and each side used dozens of historians, sociologists, psychologists, educators, and other experts. Both sides argued about highly arcane matters, the specifics of congressional debates held in 1866, and whether it was good science to use light and dark dolls to prove that segregated education affected the self-image of African American children. At the end of one particularly long and difficult day, James Nabrit stood before the Court and expressed what might be the most important and surely the most succinct point of the case: "The basic question here is one of liberty," and you "either have it or you do not."[6]

The Court ruled that separate education was implicitly unequal and that since "education is perhaps the most important function of the state and local governments," where government provides it, "it is a right which must be made available to all on equal terms."[7] And here it was—simple, clear, undeniable, and logical. Nabrit saw *liberty* as the real moral issue, but the Court recognized the real legal issue to be *equality*. And here too is the crux of the issue for deaf and hard of hearing children—if the state provides education to all, then education must be equal for all. When a deaf or hard of hearing child is denied the right to access communication in a classroom, is openly denied the right to a placement in which he or she can easily and directly communicate with classmates and teachers, when an interpreter cannot hear well enough to do his or her job, when language skills are not taught, the most basic aspects of an education are placed beyond the reach of these children, not unlike a quality education was placed beyond the hopes of African American children. Yet the *Rowley* decision (the deaf and hard of hearing child's *Plessy*) has remained intact since 1982, ensuring that the unequal treatment of these children continues every day of the school year.[8]

NOTES

1. Richard Kluger, *Simple Justice* (New York: Vintage Books, 1975), 165.

2. *Brown v. Board of Education,* 347 U.S. 483, 493 (1954).

3. *Serrano v. Priest,* 5 Cal. 3d 584, 605 (1971).

4. *Plessy v. Ferguson,* 163 U.S. 537 (1896).

5. Kluger, *Simple Justice,* 609.

6. *Id.* at 583.

7. *Brown,* 347 U.S. at 493.

8. *Board of Education v. Rowley,* 458 U.S. 176 (1982). For a discussion of the case and the Supreme Court's decision, see chapter 1.

8

EQUAL PROTECTION AND THE PLACE OF EDUCATION IN AMERICAN SOCIETY

We dissect nature along lines laid down by our native language. Language is not simply a reporting device for experience, but a defining framework for it.

—Benjamin Lee Whorf,
Language, Thought, and Reality

THERE IS A MOMENT in the classroom, one that is repeated a dozen times there, a hundred times in the school, a hundred thousand times in the district, a million times during that day throughout the country. A moment in which a thought or belief or a bit of nonsense is exchanged. A moment when one student laughs at another, then offhandedly suggests another meet her later after school. A moment when one student asks a friend how to solve a particular mathematical equation. A moment when one student says to the teacher that Shakespeare seems dumb. Moments that one thinks little about after the exchanges are completed. Moments so simple and ordinary that almost all the students in that classroom (and their peers around the nation) cannot imagine what it would be like to miss out on them. Here are a few examples.

The teacher asked her class how they would feel if the Joad family in the *Grapes of Wrath* moved in next door. The class discussed issues of poverty, prejudice, and class animosity. Karl Marx, Father Coughlin, Rush Limbaugh, and Martin Luther King Jr. entered the debate. Questions of wealth and the relationship between work and the value assigned to work were considered. Some of the students believed that the Joads had no right to complain about their lot in life. Others argued that some people start with so much more than others and that the system is, therefore, inherently unfair. "Unfair," some repeated. "Who said it should be fair?" the teacher asked. "Is it fair that a man who gets up at three o'clock in the morning and works all day lifting garbage pails should make ten dollars an hour, while someone who sells companies and moves stock around makes a thousand dollars an hour? Where is the logic or justice to that?" It was a heated but provocative discussion. It wasn't clear how many minds were changed.

The twenty-five second graders were working at their desks on a simple reading assignment. Still, there was a classroom buzz, a confluence of the noise and movement that children make. They looked like those ships one sees far out on the horizon, bobbing up and down, not fully distinct, but active and moving. The teacher sat at his desk, occasionally looking up, answering a question, quieting down another student. Finally, he looked up and half laughed, half spoke, "Well, how do you like the way the cow talked to the moon?" The children laughed, and then a dozen hands shot up into the air.

After the speeches and the band music and the standard well-wishing from the district's superintendent, the entire senior class stood and moved the tassels on their mortarboards. The cheering and crying began in the gym. Students hugged and promised to keep in touch. Everyone was talking, and the room was alive with the collective joy of the group as the students prepared to go out into the world as adults.

All these moments, rich and important, are unavailable, either partially or fully, to the deaf or hard of hearing student because there is no interpreter or the interpreter is unskilled, because the student is inappropriately placed in an environment in which he or she has no peers with whom to communicate or in which he or she cannot communicate with the teacher. So much is lost.

SERRANO V. PRIEST AND THE CONSTITUTIONAL RIGHT TO AN EDUCATION

Americans are prone to assert a right to many things that in fact are not protected by law or the Constitution. "There ought to be a law!" we cry, but that's not always true. The right to an education, though, is certainly a sacred and compulsory one in our nation, and we will go a long way to protect it. Until 1971, California's educational funding system was based primarily on local property taxes, which meant that schools in wealthy areas were much better off financially than schools in poorer areas. For example, Baldwin Park spent $577.49 per pupil annually, compared with $1,231 per pupil annually in Beverly Hills. Property valuation per pupil was $3,706 in Baldwin Park and $50,885 in Beverly Hills. Beverly Hills had a lot more money to spend on its students than Baldwin Park.[1]

Los Angeles County school children and their parents filed a lawsuit alleging that such funding inequities violated the equal protection clause. The California Supreme Court in *Serrano v. Priest* ruled that the property-tax basis for school funding in California was unconstitutional because education is a "fundamental right" and there was no "compelling" state reason for maintaining the discriminatory funding system. Thirty-plus years later, there is still debate as to whether *Serrano* really changed anything, but what is indisputable is the manner in which the California Supreme Court analyzed education and applied equal protection concepts. And because of the radical and systemic way in which an "unfair," but not previously illegal or consciously discriminatory, process was changed, millions of students and billions of dollars were affected. When it came to the education of California students, money—even the legal accumulation by some, but not others—was no justification for maintaining an unequal system.

The California Supreme Court ruled that a distinction based on wealth, although the poor were not a traditional "suspect class," would be subject to "strict scrutiny" for something as important as education. The funding scheme, the court asserted, "invidiously discriminates against the poor because it makes the quality of a child's education a function of the wealth of his parents and neighbors."[2] The court rejected outcomes based on wealth because to "allot more educational dollars to the children of one district than to those of another merely because of the fortuitous presence of such property is to make the quality of a child's education dependent upon the location of private and industrial establishments."[3]

There are several intriguing aspects of the court's treatment of lower-income communities as a suspect class as it relates to deaf and hard of hearing children. First, the establishment of the property-based funding mechanism was not a conscious effort to discriminate against children from poorer neighborhoods. Unlike the exclusion of millions of children with disabilities from any kind of meaningful education before the passage of the IDEA in 1975 or the de jure segregation of African American children before 1954, the pre-1971 California funding scheme had almost a benign quality. It was merely a reflection of wealth patterns; certainly, no one insidiously set up this funding structure. And yet the consequences of the funding system were harmful, and so the court voided it. To the extent that programs for deaf and hard of hearing children also do not reflect a conscious or mean-spirited effort to deny them communication, the issue, as in *Serrano,* is not motive but consequence.

Second, the court was moved by the fact that something fully beyond a child's control—where he or she lives—would substantively and fortuitously determine the quality of education. Are deaf and hard of hearing children no more or less fortuitously situated? Has fate left them with any greater control?

And behind it all was the recognition by the *Serrano* court, like the U.S. Supreme Court in *Brown,* of the singular importance of education. "Education plays [an indispensable role] in the modern industrial state. . . . Education is a major determinant of an individual's chance for economic and social success in our competitive society [and] is a unique influence on a child's development as a citizen and his participation in political and community life."[4] Moreover, "unequal education . . . leads to unequal job opportunities, disparate income, and handicapped ability to participate in the social, cultural, and political activity of our society."[5]

The California legislature was required to provide *one* system applicable to all schools and children; the educational system had to be uniform. Think of the importance of communication in a classroom, then consider its role in ensuring that schools are, as the California Supreme Court stated, "doorways opening into chambers of science, art, and the learned professions, as well as into fields of industrial and commercial activities"—for education "surely means more than [mere] access to the classroom."[6]

The California Supreme Court also noted, as federal courts have, that education is the "unifying social force and the basic tool for shaping democratic values . . . 'at once the symbol of our democracy and the most pervasive means for promoting our common destiny.'"[7] Education, unlike almost any other national institution, save perhaps the IRS, "is universally relevant[,] . . . continues over a lengthy period of life[,] . . . has a sustained, intensive contact with the recipient," and is unmatched in the extent to which it "molds the personality of the youth of society."[8]

The California Supreme Court understood as well the almost coercive nature of education, emphasizing both that the state made it compulsory and that public education "actively attempts to shape a child's personal development in a manner chosen not by the child or his parents but by the state."[9] It is difficult to understand why an inequality in wealth as it affects educational opportunities is more significant than an inequality in the provision of communication and language access as it affects educational opportunities for deaf and hard of hearing children. If indeed education is central to the maintenance of our democracy and the healthy maturation of our children, is mandatory, and attempts to shape our children as society deems appropriate, the state must provide deaf and hard of hearing children equal access to communication

and language as surely as the children in Baldwin Park were entitled to the same resources as the children of Beverly Hills.

THE *PLYLER* DECISION AND LITERACY
AND "INNOCENT" CHILDREN

In *Plyler v. Doe*, the U.S. Supreme Court was asked to rule on a
1975 Texas law that specifically withheld state funds for the education of children who were not legally admitted into the United
States. The Texas legislature was concerned with the increasing
population of Mexican nationals, especially because many of these
students had special education needs. Texas argued before the high
court that requiring expenditures for illegal aliens would reduce
funding available for "legal" children.

The Supreme Court referred to these illegal immigrants as our
"shadow population" numbering in the millions, a "source of
cheap labor," and an "underclass" that "presents most difficult
problems for a Nation that prides itself on adherence to principles
of equality under the law."[10] In ruling that the Texas legislation
violated the equal protection clause of the Fourteenth Amendment,
the Supreme Court stated that

> public education is not a "right" granted to individuals
> by the Constitution. . . . But neither is it merely some
> governmental "benefit" indistinguishable from other
> forms of social welfare legislation. Both the importance
> of education in maintaining our basic institutions, and
> the lasting impact of its deprivation on the life of the
> child, mark the distinction. The "American people have
> always regarded education and [the] acquisition of
> knowledge as matters of supreme importance."[11]

Having again acknowledged the central role of education, the
Supreme Court concluded that the denial of education to "select

groups" of children was "an affront to one of the goals of the Equal Protection Clause: the abolition of governmental barriers presenting unreasonable obstacles to advancement on the basis of individual merit."[12] Calling illiteracy an "enduring disability," the Court stated that the "inability to read and write will handicap the individual deprived of a basic education each and every day of his life."* The Court could not reconcile the requirements of the Fourteenth Amendment and the "inestimable toll" of educational deprivation on the "social, economic, intellectual, and psychological well-being of the individual."[13]

Finally, the Court noted in particular the nature of the group affected by the discriminatory governmental action.

> Section 21.031 [of the Texas law] imposes a lifetime hardship on a discrete class of children *not accountable for their disabling status.* The stigma of *illiteracy* will mark them for the rest of their lives. By denying these children a *basic* education, we deny them the ability to live within the structure of our civic institutions, and foreclose any realistic possibility that they will contribute in even the smallest way to the progress of our Nation. In determining the rationality [of the Texas law under the Fourteenth Amendment], we may appropriately take into account its costs to the Nation and to the *innocent children* who are its victims.[14]

I have highlighted terms in this quote because they are so apt for deaf and hard of hearing children. Although the difference between no education at all and a language-limited education should

---

*The *Plyler* Court refused to rule that education is a "fundamental" right, and so the "strict scrutiny" standard was not imposed. Instead the *Plyler* Court, unlike the California Supreme Court in *Serrano,* required only that Texas demonstrate a rational basis for its statute denying education to certain children. Texas was not able to demonstrate a rational basis for the law, and thus the Court ruled the statute unconstitutional.

not be glossed over, they represent two situations at the wrong end of the education continuum, neither acceptable, both an affront to our Constitution. In both cases children are the victims through no fault of their own, and in both cases they are denied very basic aspects of an education. The children of illegal aliens were stopped at the front door of the school. Deaf and hard of hearing children are allowed in, but in many cases they might as well be outside. That Amy Rowley was denied at least 40 percent of classroom communication was ultimately a denial of a "basic" education. That deaf and hard of hearing children finish school, if at all, with a third-grade reading level suggests the very "stigma of illiteracy" the *Plyler* Court found fundamentally unacceptable.

Deaf and hard of hearing children have not brought about their communication difference. They are not asking for something that other students are not entitled to. Whether consciously or not, our educational system has visited burdens upon them that no parent of a hearing child would or should tolerate, and the imposition of such "disabilities on the child is contrary to the basic concept of our system that legal burdens should bear some relationship to individual responsibility or wrongdoing."[15]

There is a clear and forceful right to be educated and to be educated equally. This certainly applies to the basic and necessary components of a public education: facilities, curricula, materials, and opportunities must be equal for all children so that they can access subject matter and have the opportunity to develop all necessary academic and cognitive skills, complete required academic work, and participate in school activities.

As I have noted, the denial of this right takes many forms, whether a lack of necessary support services, a lack of access to language-rich programs, or a lack of assistance in developing the required language skills to benefit from an education. This is a complicated matter, since hearing loss is a low-incidence condition and school districts cannot create critical masses of deaf and hard of hearing children. And yet the school system continues to enforce a law that discourages the very language access that our First and Fourteenth Amendments require and that, wittingly or unwittingly, erects barriers between these children and language and communication.

Systemic failure and denial of equal protection also occurs when school systems fail to assist deaf and hard of hearing children in developing their own individual communication skills. Literacy happens to a large degree in, and because of, schools. Hearing children usually come to school with established language skills. That there is no mandated provision of language- and communication-development programs for deaf and hard of hearing children to help them become literate and effective learners is further proof of a denial of equal protection.

Would a group of hearing children rightfully claim an equal protection denial if their school system did not provide a reading program to them but provided such a program to all others? If another group was denied a math program or physical education or a science curriculum, would they rightfully and forcefully call on the Fourteenth Amendment to resolve the problem?

Whatever the cause, the results are clear: many deaf and hard of hearing children are isolated in crowded classrooms, lost—fully or to a large degree—to the flow of knowledge and communication around them. The isolation of a child in a crowded classroom, cut off from information, is a fundamental and heartbreaking condition and is a denial of the equal protection that our Fourteenth Amendment guarantees.

NOTES

1. *Serrano v. Priest,* 5 Cal. 3d 584 (1971).
2. *Id.* at 589.
3. *Id.* at 601.
4. *Id.* at 605.
5. *Id.* at 606 (quoting *San Francisco Unified School District v. Johnson,* 3 Cal. 3d 937, 950 (1971)).

6. *Id.* at 607.

7. *Id.* at 608 (quoting *McCollum v. Board of Education,* 333 U.S. 203, 231 (1948)).

8. *Id.* at 609–610.

9. *Id.* at 610.

10. *Plyler v. Doe,* 457 U.S. 202, 218–219 (1982).

11. *Id.* at 221 (quoting *Meyer v. Nebraska,* 262 U.S. 390, 400 (1923)).

12. *Id.* at 221–222.

13. *Id.* at 222.

14. *Id.* at 223–224 (emphasis added).

15. *Weber v. Aetna Casualty & Surety Co.,* 406 U.S. 164, 175 (1972).

9

EQUAL PROTECTION AND THE RIGHT TO COMMUNICATION AND LANGUAGE

Language is a part of our organism and no less complicated than it.

—Ludwig Wittgenstein, *Notebooks, 1914–1916*

I worked extra hard in my high school art class because I thought art was one thing I could do on my own, and I really liked it. However, I never got over a D, and most of the time it was an F. I never understood this. When I would ask for help, the teacher would say she was too busy. One day, I went to class early and saw her telling another person that she hated when they put special education students in her class, so she automatically failed them. I was so hurt, I gave up my dream for art.

I had a fifth grade teacher who really didn't care if I didn't understand what she was teaching. She always moved around the classroom or faced the blackboard when she spoke. I remember reminding her to turn around to face me when she spoke. She responded, "If you didn't hear what I said . . . Tough!"

My worst teacher in grade school didn't care that I was deaf. He sat me in the back of the room where I couldn't possibly see him. He talked while facing the chalkboard so I could never speech-read him, and he talked so fast that I would never understand what he was saying. He made me feel worthless. He made me feel like being deaf was a disease that he didn't want to catch. The experience turned me off to teachers for a while, as well as to education.

Probably one of the most painful of my experiences was taking a major spelling test and flunking because I could not lip-read single words out of context. After I tried to tell the teacher of my predicament, she scolded me in front of the entire class and then picked a peer to read the words to me in the back of the room during a retake. Because the class was still in session, she whispered the words to me. Needless to say, I flunked the spelling test even though I knew how to spell every single word.

The worst experience I ever had was with a junior high basketball coach. From the beginning of the year, he never showed an interest in helping me. I remember going through the year in a daze of confusion, never really sure what was going on. When my parents came into school for a special meeting to express their concerns, he commented, "She hears what she wants to hear." He insisted that I was too smart to be deaf and that I was playing with everyone, audiological evidence to the contrary.

One day, I missed something she said. She approached me and told me to sit properly. I complied, but she uttered the word "deaf-mute" in the most demeaning way. The class laughed at me. With this public humiliation, I felt this rage burning inside me. . . . The years have passed, but I still have this rage against that woman.[1]

The Importance of, and Right to, Language: An Overview and History

IF THE COURTS have applied the Fourteenth Amendment's equal protection clause to a child's right to an education, what of an individual's more specific right to his or her language? In order to discuss bilingual rights (chapter 10), I must note the significant difference between "new" Americans learning English but maintaining their native language when they have the aural and oral capacity to master both and deaf and hard of hearing individuals whose capacity to learn English orally and aurally may be in question. This difference makes the matter of a right to, and the need for, one's native language that much more dramatic for deaf and hard of hearing children.

Americans are generally interested in language, whether it appears in the form of referenda to make English the official (and only) language or in the form of laws and programs that recognize and protect non-English languages. It is a curious push-pull because language defines, and is necessary for the continuation of, distinct cultures within American subcommunities, and yet there is pressure to melt Spanish and Vietnamese and all the other languages into our American English, without much thought as to the value of language and community. The nineteenth-century playwright Israel Zangwill wrote of the American melting pot, a dubious notion at best, for we sense in our bones the importance of maintaining that which defines our own communities— whether it be pride in being from Ireland or Kenya or Laos, or speaking Spanish or Russian or Swahili. And although some dubiously condemn those they claim don't want to learn English and become Americans, we rue the loss of those language-rich and culturally different neighborhoods of the nineteenth and twentieth centuries.

Do we prefer that all "language minorities be transformed into monolingual English speakers," or do we want a society in which "linguistic difference [can] be accommodated and multilingualism be embraced as a public asset"? Language creates a "strong correlation to personhood," and "language acquisition" and language itself are "phenomena woven into the fabric of ethnic communities and their people."[2] As of 2001, 10 percent of the total school-age population in America was composed of children whose native language was other than English.[3] Clearly, this percentage is on the rise; from 1979 to 1999, the population of five- to twenty-four-year olds increased 6 percent, whereas the number of members of that age group who spoke a language other than English increased 118 percent, from 6.3 million to 13.7 million.[4]

By 1990, 32 million individuals over the age of five spoke a language other than English at home—14 percent of the total U.S. population. By 2004, that figure was nearly 50 million, or 18 percent of the U.S. population, with 32 percent of that group speaking Spanish as their primary language.[5] There are approximately 155 languages spoken in America, including Spanish, Chinese, Hebrew, Aleut, Achumawi, Apache, Clallam, Hidatsa, Farsi, and Albanian. Approximately 3.5 million children spoke Spanish, 11,000 spoke French, 37,000 spoke Russian, and 88,000 spoke Vietnamese in American K–12 schools.[6]

There is of course a tension between the importance of maintaining one's native language and culture, including historic national and family ties, and the importance of developing the English skills necessary to function fully in American society. However, developing English skills need not be at the expense of losing one's native language. Accommodating bilingual skills will help "counter the sense of alienation that linguistic and ethnic minorities feel from mainstream politics and social life," and "acceptance of multilingualism as an asset will help bring people who might otherwise disengage from public institutions into the public sphere, serving the interest of broad and equal participation." Bilingual individuals "inhabit two communities" and can "serve as a bridge to bring those communities together."[7]

If we can understand the importance of multilingual communities who can hear English, then we can surely understand how the issue of language access and language rights applies to deaf and hard of hearing children (and adults). A deaf person whose first language is ASL is singularly and powerfully tied to her linguistic community and culture, particularly given the limitations of meaningful access to the "hearing" world. Developing written English is both crucial for deaf and hard of hearing people and fully consistent with maintaining their native language.

As I discussed in chapters 7 and 8, any laws, policies, or procedures that distinguish on the basis of race, nationality, or religion or affect our fundamental rights are going to raise serious equal protection concerns and will more often than not be judged unconstitutional. We understand that there are other distinctions—gender, for example—that also raise important constitutional concerns and issues of equal protection application. What about distinctions based on communication mode or language and equal protection?

In eighteenth- and particularly nineteenth-century America, bilingualism was a fact of life, positively reflected in laws and state constitutions. Ohio, for example, explicitly authorized bilingual education. In California and New Mexico, there were English and Spanish schools; and in Louisiana, French-language public schools. Throughout the Midwest there were German-, Czech-, Dutch-, Norwegian-, and Lithuanian-language schools. In the mid-nineteenth century, Minnesota issued its state constitution in five different languages. From 1805 to 1850, Pennsylvania laws were published in English and German, and in Louisiana laws were published in English and French. The 1849 California Constitution was published in English and Spanish.[8]

This kind of bi- or multilingualism began to change at the end of the nineteenth century. By 1900, California and New Mexico had English-only schools; by the 1920s, thirty-four states had laws establishing English-only schools. American education began to reflect a simple "sink or swim" approach in which non-English-speaking students were placed in English classes where they would either develop necessary English skills or not.[9]

With the civil rights movement of the 1950s and 1960s came attitudinal, policy, and legal changes that reflected, to some degree, a greater sensitivity toward language minorities. The Voting Rights Act of 1965 was amended in 1975 to require the distribution of bilingual voting material, including ballots in Spanish, Chinese,

Japanese, Korean, specific Native American languages, and Eskimo.[10] In enacting this law, the U.S. Congress found that

> voting discrimination against citizens of language minorities is pervasive and national in scope. Such minority citizens are from environments in which the dominant language is other than English. In addition they have been denied equal educational opportunities by State and local governments, resulting in severe disabilities and continuing illiteracy in the English language. The Congress further finds that, where State and local officials conduct elections only in English, language minority citizens are excluded from participating in the electoral process. . . . The Congress declares that, in order to enforce the guarantees of the fourteenth and fifteenth amendments to the United States Constitution, it is necessary to eliminate such discrimination by prohibiting English-only elections, and by prescribing other remedial devices.[11]

Federal law has been enacted to protect the voting rights of language minorities, to establish bilingual programs for those whose first language is not English, to require language interpreters in courtrooms, and to mandate the use of foreign languages in federally funded immigrant and community health centers as well as federally funded alcohol-abuse centers.[12]

Keeping in mind the constitutional standards for equal protection, numerous courts have viewed language as tantamount to that immutable characteristic that requires the highest constitutional protection. In a case involving bilingual jurors, the U.S. Supreme Court recognized that "it may well be, for certain ethnic groups and in some communities, that proficiency in a particular language, like skin color, should be treated as a surrogate for race under an equal protection analysis."[13]

A municipal rule that employees could speak only English in

the workplace, except when serving Spanish-speaking clients, was found to be discriminatory because language was the same as "national origin" and therefore subject to the greatest protection.

> In the United States, persons of Asian and Spanish origin constitute large minorities [and] regularly communicate in a language other than English. . . . Members of these minority groups have made great contributions to the development of our diverse multicultural society and its tradition of encouraging the free exchange of ideas. . . . Because language and accents are identifying characteristics, rules which have a negative effect on bilinguals, individuals with accents, or non-English speakers may be mere pretexts for intentional national origin discrimination.[14]

The same court also wrote that the "multicultural character of American society has a long and venerable history and is widely recognized as one of the United States' greatest strengths" and that although an "individual may learn English and become assimilated into American society, his primary language remains an important link to his ethnic culture and identity," which in turn "not only conveys certain concepts, but is itself an affirmation of that culture." The court held, therefore, that English-only rules should be "closely scrutinized," for they can "create an atmosphere of inferiority, isolation, and intimidation."[15] In another language-related case, the court said that "to a person who speaks only one tongue or to a person who has difficulty using another language than the one spoken in his home, language might well be an immutable characteristic like skin color, sex, or place of birth."[16] That would certainly apply to many deaf and hard of hearing children.

Another court noted its concerns with "rules which use language as a means of isolating a particular group" and recognized the need for courts to look very carefully at situations in which "vulnerable" language groups are threatened "with the deprivation of an important right." The court concluded with a concern that is directly applicable to deaf and hard of hearing students: "Plaintiff, as a member of a minority language group . . . is vulnerable to the vagaries of majoritarian politics. . . . The use of one's language is an important aspect of one's ethnicity, and should not be sacrificed to government or business interests without good cause."[17]

Native language matters, communities based on language matter, and the Constitution and our laws protect those languages and communities. Can it be less so for deaf people, who not only have a distinct language but a well-defined community based on that language and a disconnect from the hearing world that is wholly unique?

When we turn to educational law, policy, and programs, we see more clearly the failure to provide for the language and educational needs of deaf and hard of hearing students and thus the inherent applicability of the Fourteenth Amendment's equal protection clause to those programs and those students. If the highest level of protection under the Fourteenth Amendment is available for non-English-speaking hearing citizens, it is difficult to justify not applying the same protection to deaf and hard of hearing children. When Amy Rowley was denied an interpreter, her inherent right to language under the Fourteenth Amendment was also denied. Deaf and hard of hearing children should not be treated differently from other Americans whose language is rightfully protected by our laws.

NOTES

1. All the vignettes are reprinted from Gina A. Oliva, *Alone in the Mainstream* (Washington, D.C.: Gallaudet University Press, 2002), 44–46.

2. Christina M. Rodriguez, "Accommodating Linguistic Difference: Toward a Comprehensive Theory of Language Rights in the United States," *Harvard Civil Rights–Civil Liberties Law Review* 36 (2001): 136, 142.

3. Melanie Gurley Keeney and Stephanie Tueth, "Legal Issues Involving Educating Children with Limited English Proficiency," National School

Boards Association, http://www.nsba.org/site/doc_cosa.asp?TrackID=&SID=1&DID=11273&CID=164&VID=50.

4. U.S. Department of Education, National Center for Education Statistics, *The Condition of Education 2003*, NCES 2003–067 (Washington, D.C., 2003), 21, http://nces.ed.gov/pubs2003/2003067.pdf.

5. U.S. Department of Education, National Center for Education Statistics, *Issue Brief: English Language Learner Students in U.S. Public Schools: 1994 and 2000*, NCES 2004–035, August 2004, 1, http://nces.ed.gov/pubs2004/2004035.pdf.

6. *Id.*; Mary Kent and Robert Lalasz, "In the News: Speaking English in the United States," Population Reference Bureau, http://www.prb.org/Articles/2006/IntheNewsSpeakingEnglishintheUnitedStates.aspx.

7. Rodriguez, "Accommodating Linguistic Difference," 148.

8. "Official English: Federal Limits on Efforts to Curtail Bilingual Services in the States," *Harvard Law Review* 100 (1987): 1345, 1346.

9. Marguerite Malakoff and Kenji Hakuta, "History of Language Minority Education in the United States," in *Bilingual Education: Issues and Strategies*, ed. Amado M. Padilla, Halford H. Fairchild, and Concepcion M. Valadez (Newbury Park, Calif.: Sage, 1990).

10. 42 U.S.C. § 1973b(f)(1) (1982); S. Rep. No. 94–295, at 29, *as reprinted in* 1975 U.S.C.C.A.N. 774, 796.

11. 42 U.S.C. § 1973b(f)(1) (1982).

12. 42 U.S.C. §§ 1971–1974; 20 U.S.C. §§ 3281–3341; 28 U.S.C. § 1827(d); 42 U.S.C. § 454b(f)(3)(j); 42 U.S.C. § 577 (b)(3).

13. *Hernandez v. New York*, 500 U.S. 352, 371 (1991).

14. *Gutierrez v. Municipal Court*, 838 F.2d 1031, 1038–1039 (9th Cir. 1988), *vacated as moot*, 490 U.S. 1016 (1989).

15. *Id.* at 1039–1040.

16. *Garcia v. Gloor*, 618 F.2d. 264, 270 (5th Cir. 1980), *cert. denied*, 449 U.S. 1113 (1982).

17. *Smothers v. Benitez*, 806 F. Supp. 299, 309 (D.P.R. 1992).

10

~

THE APPLICATION
OF BILINGUAL-EDUCATION LAW
AND PROGRAMS TO DEAF
AND HARD OF HEARING STUDENTS

A language is a horizon.

—Roland Barthes, "What Is Writing?"
in *Writing Degree Zero*

By the time Sharon was twelve months old, her parents sensed that something was amiss, but Sharon's pediatrician assured her parents that Sharon had met all her developmental milestones and would be fine. By eighteen months, Sharon was still not responding to environmental sounds, so her parents took her back to the doctor, who suggested further testing but also suggested that Sharon might be retarded. Sharon's parents then went to a specialist, who informed them that Sharon was profoundly and irreversibly deaf. She had just turned two and a half.

Although Sharon's parents were shocked and even depressed, they soon began to research the matter. They contacted local support groups and talked to other families with deaf children. At first, they hoped she could be taught to communicate like a hearing child. They worked with a speech therapist who gave them strategies to help Sharon learn to recognize and produce spoken language, to read lips. At age three, Sharon was placed in an oral program, but by five, she had developed few, if any, expressive or receptive language skills, had no pre-reading skills, and acted out constantly. When she wanted something, she would scream and hit the table, the walls, anything nearby, including herself. There were too many days when her mother or father stood nearby, asking Sharon, over and over, slowly and loudly, "What? Tell us what you want."

Finally, out of pure desperation, Sharon's parents attended a conference of a national organization of families with deaf and hard of hearing children. Sharon's parents were immediately struck by the constant movement of the children. They ran everywhere, but more importantly, they were signing to each other, to the adults, to anyone within eyeshot. Sharon's parents went outside and cried.

During the second day of the conference, Sharon's parents attended a workshop on language development. The speaker, a deaf individual who taught at Gallaudet University in Washington, D.C.—the only liberal arts university for deaf people in the world—carefully explained how every child, hearing or deaf, needed a native language base, whether Spanish or English or ASL. She explained that studies increasingly showed that it did not matter whether a baby first developed sign language or oral language. The key was having a formal language base from which the child could then learn English and become literate. She explained that ASL was the natural and formal language of deaf people and that when they developed ASL skills, particularly at an early age, they generally did as well in school as their hearing peers, all other things being equal. When Sharon's parents left the workshop, they saw Sharon on the playground standing with two other deaf children, who eagerly signed to her and at one point, even took her hand to form a sign.

When Sharon was six, her parents took her to a language assessment center affiliated with the local medical school and university. The center's findings were clear: Sharon needed to develop ASL as quickly as possible. Her parents took a deep breath and enrolled Sharon in a program associated with the center. She slowly but surely began to learn ASL. Sharon's parents also began to learn ASL, not an easy task given its visual nature and different grammatical structure. But slowly they learned enough to communicate with their daughter. Her tantrums stopped, and more importantly, they saw her smile.

At Sharon's next IEP meeting, the school administrator reviewed all the reports, including those from the center. "I must be honest with you. I am usually fairly sure, even before the meeting, what every one of my children need. But not today. It is clear Sharon is not developing oral-aural skills, and so it would be my recommendation that she not continue in our oral program."

Sharon's mother responded, "We agree. Sharon has been without language for six years. It isn't anyone's fault. We hoped, we prayed, we struggled, to help her develop oral language because we want our daughter to function and be happy in a hearing world. We want her to be at the family Thanksgiving and Christmas parties and to be able to talk to her grandparents and her cousins—"

Sharon's mother paused, regrouped, and continued. "But that is a false hope. We knew it every day we watched as Sharon kicked and screamed when she wanted a glass of milk but had no way to tell us that. But now she is developing ASL, and the center is adamant that she be exposed to that every day in school, that she have someone who can work with her on those skills. Every day."

"Have you thought about the state school?"

"Yes, but she is only six, and more importantly, we feel she needs to develop a stronger language base, develop a greater sense of herself, be more comfortable socially before we take the big step of moving her three hundred miles away from home. We think she'll be ready in a year or two. I've done a lot of reading on this and have made copies of the studies on ASL and developing literacy. Let me pass those around."

The team looked at each other as the administrator took his copy.

"We appreciate that and we'll read them. But until she goes to the state school—and by the way, we cannot formally commit to that until you are ready, and of course there is no guarantee now about what might be right down the road—we want to help her now."

"Good," the mother replied. "Sharon needs at least ninety minutes a day of intense ASL instruction, needs an ASL interpreter for her classes. Because there are no other students who use ASL in the school or even in any nearby schools, we are arranging for her to go to a program in the county where other profoundly deaf children meet after school and on the weekends."

The pause was uncomfortably long. Finally, the administrator suggested a break. Sharon's parents watched as he and his staff went into a nearby room and closed the door. They returned in twenty minutes.

"We support your after-school plans. As to Sharon's daily program, we are prepared to offer the following. She can remain in her current program or be placed in the regular second-grade class. If you choose the latter, we will provide her with three hours a week of interpretation. In addition, the interpreter will work with Sharon on her ASL skills one hour a week."

"Will it be a qualified ASL interpreter, and is the interpreter qualified to teach my daughter ASL?"

The administrator saw the disappointment on the parents' faces, but did not answer the question.

"In the alternative, we are prepared to place her in the county's communicationally handicapped class."

"Tell us about that class."

"Well, there are twenty-one children. Most are hearing impaired. I think four are autistic, and one or two are emotionally disturbed. The teacher has been in the district for eighteen years and has worked with many deaf and hard of hearing students."

"Does she sign?"

"She knows some signs."

"ASL?"

"I'd have to check."

"Probably not?

"No, probably not."

"And even if she knows some ASL, is she fluent?"

"No."

"Is there an interpreter?"

"There is no need for one since the teacher knows some signs."

"Mr. Harris, if we place Sharon in that class, will she be able to use or learn ASL in any meaningful way?"

"Folks, I have to be honest with you. If you don't place Sharon in the state school, there is no way we can provide ASL in that class."

"Then you have to hire someone who can communicate with her in the language she needs to be a literate person, to be able to communicate with her peers."

The administrator looked around the table, waited for others to say something, and then closed the meeting by saying, "I'm sorry, we are not required to provide ASL instruction. We believe the options we've provided meet the legal requirements. If you are willing to place Sharon in the state school, we will not object."*

WHAT IS AMERICAN LAW regarding the right of students in public schools to have equal access to their native language or communication system, and why doesn't it apply to deaf and hard of hearing children? Although there have been challenges to our

*This vignette is a composite of various stories and recollections of my clients and colleagues.

bilingual educational system, there are effective bilingual programs for millions of students in the United States whose native language is other than English. These are children who can hear and are capable of learning spoken English, but who, nonetheless, are provided specific programs in English and their native language to ensure that they are fully educated. Why such programs are not provided to children who have a different native language—ASL—and who have a reduced or no capacity to hear is an important question. If the equal protection clause of the Fourteenth Amendment has any meaning and value, it requires the provision of bilingual programs for deaf and hard of hearing children so that they can both access and develop communication and language, the central ingredients to any educational progress.

Public schools "are legally mandated to provide an equal opportunity education for language-minority students. School districts must provide not only English language education, but also general curriculum instruction in the students' native languages."[1] Congress enacted the Bilingual Education Act (BEA) in 1968, which allocated funds for bilingual projects and programs so that "where inability to speak and understand English excludes national origin minority group children from effective participation in the educational program . . . the district must take affirmative steps to rectify the language deficiency."[2]

Despite the enactment of the BEA, bilingual-education law did not become meaningful until the 1974 U.S. Supreme Court decision in *Lau v. Nichols,* a class-action lawsuit brought on behalf of more than 2,800 Chinese American students in San Francisco who did not speak, understand, read, or write English. Of those students, 1,800 received no services "to deal with this language deficiency."[3] The Court ruled that the failure of the San Francisco Unified School District to provide instruction in the students' native language raised equal protection questions. At the time of this litigation, section 71 of the California Education Code provided that "English shall be the basic language of instruction in all schools" and that all pupils will have a "mastery of English." The *Lau* Court concluded that

> basic English skills are at the very core of what these public schools teach. Imposition of a requirement that, before a child can effectively participate in the educational program, he must already have acquired those basic skills is to make a mockery of public education. We know that those who do not understand English are certain to find their classroom experiences wholly incomprehensible and in no way meaningful.[4]

The *Lau* Court ruled that "the Chinese-speaking minority receive fewer benefits than the English-speaking majority from respondents' school system which denies them a meaningful opportunity to participate in the educational program."[5] The Court's analysis clearly applies to deaf and hard of hearing students, whose own language access, as well as access to the larger educational curricula, is certainly as questionable as that of the Chinese American students in San Francisco, particularly given the more limited ability of deaf and hard of hearing students to develop spoken English, an ability that the hearing students in the *Lau* case possessed.

The U.S. Congress codified the *Lau* decision by enacting the Equal Educational Opportunity Act of 1974, which required school districts to "take appropriate action to overcome language barriers that impeded equal participation by its students in its instructional programs."[6] Bilingual-education law gives school districts programmatic discretion; the specific characteristics of the children within a given school district are used to decide whether the program will consist of English-immersion classes or true bilingual instruction. Federal law requires "an equal opportunity," including, for those children whose primary language is other than English, instruction in their native language to ensure that they learn English.

The BEA was later merged into Title VII of the Elementary and Secondary Education Act and then subsumed under the No Child Left Behind Act (NCLB) of 2001. The key provisions of the NCLB listed below have particular relevance to the communication and language needs of deaf and hard of hearing children, even though these provisions are not applied to them.

> English Language Acquisition, Language Enhancement, and Academic Achievement Act
>
> . . .
>
> Sec. 3102. Purposes.
> The purposes of this part are—
>
> . . .
>
> (3) to develop *high-quality language instruction* educational programs . . .
>
> . . .
>
> (5) to assist State educational agencies, local educational agencies, and schools to build their capacity to *establish, implement, and sustain language instruction educational programs and programs of English language development for limited English proficient children;*
>
> . . .
>
> (7) . . . to help limited English proficient children . . . develop proficiency in English, while meeting challenging State academic content and student academic achievement standards;
>
> . . .
>
> Sec. 3116. Local Plans.
>
> . . .
>
> (c) Teacher English Fluency.—Each eligible entity . . . shall include in its plan a certification that *all teachers in any language instruction educational program for limited English proficient children . . . are fluent in English and any other language used for instruction,* including having written and oral communications skills.[7]

Improving Language Instruction Educational Programs

Sec. 3202. Purpose.

The purpose of this part is to help ensure that *limited English proficient* children *master English* and meet the same rigorous standards for academic achievement as all children are expected to meet, including meeting challenging State academic context and student achievement standards *by*—

. . .

(2) *developing language skills* and multicultural understanding;

. . .

(6) developing programs that strengthen and *improve the professional training of educational personnel who work with limited English proficient children.*

The NCLB Declaration of Rights for Parents of English Language Learners set forth the following additional rights, among others, for parents and children:

- the right for a child *to learn English* and other subjects such as reading and other language arts and mathematics at the same academic level as all other students;
- the right to choose a different English-acquisition program *if one is available*;
- the right to have a child tested annually to assess his or her progress in *English-language acquisition;* and
- *the right for a child to have the opportunity to reach his or her greatest academic potential.*[8]

It is ironic that children whose primary language is other than English and are covered by bilingual-education law have the capacity to learn spoken English, whereas deaf and many hard of hearing children do not but are not covered.

Bilingual-education legislation is based on an understanding of the importance of developing English skills and maintaining culturally and linguistically distinct communities, despite any current (and historically repeated) nativistic notions that America must be a country only for English-speaking citizens. Some argue that maintaining community and language is ultimately the best way to ensure the kind of inclusion that we claim to want for all in our society.

> One need not regard integration solely or even primarily as a cultural objective. The kind of integration at the heart of fluid civic identity focuses on the removal of structural impediments to the advancement of minorities. . . . [Moreover,] if bilingual education is meant to help linguistic minorities assimilate, then assimilation depends in part on segregation. . . . [And to] the extent that our vision of equal justice depends on the rights of individuals to make choices about how to construct their communities, the ability of racial and ethnic minorities to maintain ties to their non-mainstream identities must be included in that vision. Regardless of whether bilingual education serves as an integrative device or as a means of preserving cultural difference, its existence, made necessary by the presence of linguistic minorities in the first place, underscores the cultural complexity of the total political community.[9]

This notion of using bilingual education not only to instruct children in English but also to maintain valuable community ties is, of course, directly applicable to the Deaf community, deaf schools, and other educational programs that provide a critical mass of language peers to deaf and hard of hearing children. As a group so fundamentally formed around language, deaf and hard of hearing people may gain even more from the application of true bilingual education than those for whom the law was enacted.

A brief survey of some of the court decisions related to bilingual education illuminates the direct application of equal protection to deaf and hard of hearing children who need and deserve similar programs.

CASTANEDA V. PICKARD (1981)

Approximately 85 percent of the school population in the Raymondville School District (Texas) was Mexican American. The school district operated a bilingual program for all students in kindergarten, the goal of which was to teach students fundamental reading and writing skills in both Spanish and English by the end of the third grade.[10] The district offered no bilingual programs after the third grade. The families of the Mexican American students filed suit against the district for failing to provide a full bilingual program. The trial court ruled in favor of the district, but the appellate court reversed the decision.

The appellate court found that bilingual-education law "clearly imposes on an educational agency a duty to take appropriate action to remedy the language barriers" of students and that "language grouping" is an "unobjectionable practice" because when "children [are grouped] on the basis of language for purposes of a language remediation or bilingual education," the benefits of this "segregation" outweigh the adverse effects. The court believed that it was essential to remedy the language barriers that limit a student in an English-language school.*

*The IDEA and its LRE and mainstreaming ethos discourage the placement of deaf and hard of hearing children in language-rich environments because those environments often do not include enough, or any, so-called nondisabled children. Courts have struggled with this issue,

The court found that the school district's failure to remedy language difficulties need not be a conscious one. The court also recognized that "limited English" students entered school facing a "task not encountered by students who are already proficient in English."[11]

The court expressed its considerable concern regarding the school district's failure to provide teachers who were appropriately trained and proficient in the child's language: "Any school district that chooses to fulfill its obligations [under bilingual law] by means of a bilingual-education program has undertaken a responsibility to provide teachers who are able completely to teach in such a program. The record in this case indicates that some of the teachers . . . have a very limited command of Spanish." A bilingual program will not meet its goals if the "teachers charged with the day-to-day responsibility for educating these children . . . operate under their own unremedied language disability."[12]

The court's recognition of the need for a rich language environment, teachers skilled in the student's native language, and a concentration of students who speak the same language resonates with the need of many deaf and hard of hearing students for programs in which there are language-proficient teachers and a critical mass of language peers. The *Castaneda* court's understanding here stands in sharp contrast to the case (discussed in chapter 3) in which the interpreter learned all her sign language from the student for whom she was hired to interpret and other cases in which a deaf child must remain in a school as the only signing child rather than attend a state school with hundreds of language peers. Deaf and hard of hearing students, of course, vary in their language skill levels and even in how much they rely on sign versus oral-aural language. But whatever their unique linguistic needs, they are

caught between the integrationist nature of the IDEA and the unique language needs of deaf and hard of hearing children. *See Poolaw v. Bishop,* 67 F.3d 830 (9th Cir. 1995).

entitled to develop language skills commensurate with their age and innate abilities, as were the students in *Castaneda*.

SERNA V. PORTALES MUNICIPAL SCHOOLS (1974)

A lawsuit brought against the Portales, New Mexico, school district claimed that the district failed to provide an appropriate education for Hispanic students.[13] These students knew very little English and as a result did poorly in school. Achievement tests given in English guaranteed that these students would fail. By the first or second grade, these students were one year behind in reading, language mechanics, and language expression, a disparity that increased by the fifth grade. Evidence was submitted to the court that

> when Spanish surnamed children come to school and find that their language and culture are totally rejected and that only English is acceptable, feelings of inadequacy and lowered self-esteem develop. . . . A child who goes to a school where he finds no evidence of his language and culture and ethnic group represented becomes withdrawn and nonparticipating.[14]

The failure to provide a bilingual program for these students and to "rectify language deficiencies so that these children will receive a meaningful education," required that the school system take affirmative steps to resolve the problem.[15] The school district was ordered to provide a bilingual program for students in grades one through four, including daily instruction in Spanish. If students continued to demonstrate insufficient English proficiency, the district had to continue the bilingual instruction.

CINTRON V. BRENTWOOD UNION FREE SCHOOL DISTRICT (1978)

The Brentwood, New York, school district had approximately 3,700 Hispanic students out of a total school population of

19,000.[16] The school district had a bilingual program in place, which included instruction in Spanish and exposure to English. As the students progressed from year to year, use of English in school increased and use of Spanish decreased. Parents had the choice of placing their children in English or bilingual classes. Students with limited English skills were taught English and received remedial help from teachers who would explain topics in Spanish. The court ruled that the school's bilingual program was insufficient and found that

1. it is "unlawful" to fail to take appropriate action to overcome language barriers;
2. the *Lau* decision and subsequent federal guidelines require that a school district "assess the language ability of the student," "identify the nature and extent of the student's educational needs," and "implement the type of educational programs dependent upon the degree of linguistic proficiency"; and
3. although integration of non-English-speaking students is important, the need for students to become language proficient requires that the school district use whatever placements and programs are necessary to achieve such proficiency.[17]

Accordingly, the court required that

1. the school district's bilingual plan contain specific methods for identifying children "on admission" who are deficient in the English language;
2. the school district monitor the progress of such children; and
3. the school district create a training program to ensure the bilingual skills and bicultural awareness of teachers and aides.[18]

The court's description of the school's failings and appropriate remedies are fully applicable to deaf and hard of hearing children.

GUADALUPE V. TEMPE ELEMENTARY SCHOOL DISTRICT (1972)

The defendant school district in Tempe, Arizona, was charged with failing to (1) provide Mexican American and Yaqui Indian children with bilingual instruction, (2) hire enough teachers of Mexican American or Yaqui Indian descent who could adequately teach bilingual courses and effectively relate to the educational and cultural needs of the children, and (3) structure a curriculum that took into account the children's educational and cultural needs.[19] The court cited the following about bilingual-education law, policies, and guidelines:

> The U.S. Office of Education has defined bilingual education as instruction in two languages and the use of those two languages as mediums of instruction for any part of or all of the school curriculum.
>
> In passing the Bilingual Education Act, Congress: hereby finds that one of the most acute educational problems in the United States is that which involves millions of children of limited English-speaking ability because they come from environments where the dominant language is other than English.[20]

Accordingly, Congress found that "additional efforts should be made to supplement present attempts to find adequate and constructive solutions" to the problem and that there is an "urgent need" for "comprehensive and cooperative action now on the local, State, and Federal levels to develop forward looking approaches to meet the serious learning difficulties faced by this substantial segment of the Nation's school age population."[21] With the court's acknowledgement that bilingual education is instruction in two languages, deaf and hard of hearing children seem justified in asking, where are the two-language programs for us? Where are the programs that systemically help us develop both native language skills and the ability to read and write English?*

MARTIN LUTHER KING JUNIOR ELEMENTARY SCHOOL CHILDREN V. ANN ARBOR SCHOOL DISTRICT (1979)

The Equal Educational Opportunities Act of 1974 (EEOA) provides that

> no state shall deny equal educational opportunity to an individual on account of his or her race, color, or national origin, by—
>
> . . .
>
> (f) the failure . . . to take appropriate action to overcome language barriers that impede equal participation by its students in its instructional programs.[22]

---

*There have been many other bilingual-education cases that have a direct relationship to the linguistic needs of deaf and hard of hearing children. See, for example, *Rios v. Read,* 480 F. Supp. 14 (E.D.N.Y. 1978), in which the district court found that a school district had failed to hire teachers sufficiently trained in bilingual education and had an administrator for the program who did not speak Spanish. The court stated that bilingual-education law was enacted to "assure the language-deficit child" the "same opportunity to learn as that offered his or her English speaking counterpart," that the school "cannot be allowed to compromise a student's right to meaningful education before proficiency in English is obtained," and therefore that the school had a legal obligation to take "affirmative action for language-deficient students by establishing an ESL [English as a second language] and bilingual program" and to keep the students in "such program until they have attained proficiency in English." *Id.* at 22, 23.

The EEOA is striking for at least two reasons. First, it recognizes the educational impact of "language barriers" on children. Second, it requires that schools take action to overcome those barriers. Section 1703(f) (above) refers to a denial based on "race, color, or national origin" (paralleling the suspect-class component of equal protection law); however, one must ask why deaf and hard of hearing children are not included in the law's reach. As the U.S. Supreme Court has stated, "in some communities . . . proficiency in a particular language, like skin color, should be treated as a surrogate for race" for purposes of an equal protection analysis.[23]*

There have been numerous court decisions regarding the EEOA, but one stands out for its applicability to the language and educational plight of deaf and hard of hearing children. In *Martin Luther King Jr. Elementary School Children v. Ann Arbor School District,* certain African American children spoke "black English," a black vernacular or dialect distinct in many ways from standard English. They sued the school district under section 1703(f) to force it to take appropriate action so that the children could learn standard English to use in school, in the commercial world, and in the arts, sciences, and professions.[24]

The court ruled that the school district had to develop a plan to overcome the language barriers facing these children, including training school staff to understand, identify, and assist these children in developing standard English skills. The school district was required to make use of "black English" because it "has been shown to be a distinct, definable version of English [but] different from . . . the general world of communications . . . [and] is not used by the mainstream of society—black or white."[25]

Although there is a world of difference between ASL (or even Signing Exact English or Cued Speech) and "black English," judi-

*As I noted in chapter 7, given the linguistic, cultural, and historic characteristics of the deaf and hard of hearing communities, it is not difficult to make the case that the communities should have the same Fourteenth Amendment protections as those provided to suspect classes.

cial recognition of the latter is important for deaf and hard of hearing students. ASL, Signing Exact English, Cued Speech, and "black English" are all unique community-based modes of communicating that directly affect the development of standard English skills as well as literacy and academic growth more broadly. In its ruling, the Michigan court could not have more clearly recognized the central importance of communication and language, calling the children's legal action a "cry for judicial help in opening the doors to the establishment . . . and [necessary to prevent] another generation from becoming functionally illiterate."

> A major goal of American education . . . is to train young people to communicate. . . . The art of communication among the people of the country in all aspects of people's lives is a basic building block in the development of each individual. Children need to learn to speak and understand and to read and write the language used by society to carry on its business, to develop its science, arts and culture, and to carry on its professions and governmental functions. . . . [A] major goal of a school system is to teach reading, writing, speaking and understanding standard English.[26]

In passing the EEOA, Congress intended to "set standards for *all* school districts throughout the Nation, as the basic requirements for carrying out, in the field of public education, the Constitutional guarantee that each shall have *equal protection of the laws*" and set forth the "obligation of the school system . . . to take appropriate action to overcome the *language barrier.*"[27]*

*The U.S. Office of Education has said that bilingual education should include the "study of the history and culture associated with a student's mother tongue." Deaf children have a unique history and culture directly associated with, and indeed the result of, their "mother tongue"— ASL. *Guadalupe v. Tempe Elementary School District*, 587 F.2d 1022, 1022 (9th Cir. 1978).

The court understood that a child's language barrier could not be overcome unless the system recognized the child's home language system and employed that knowledge to help the child learn standard English. The ruling reads like an analysis of the central issues facing deaf and hard of hearing children and illuminates the failure of the educational system to approach their linguistic needs with the same passion, understanding, and legal direction that drove this court to identify the core linguistic needs of those children in Michigan.

Judicial recognition of the importance of language development and proficiency is apparent from these bilingual-education cases. The clear legal obligations of schools to provide bilingual instruction, qualified bilingual teachers, and a curriculum that recognizes both is also well established. It is obvious that the courts understand the direct and unmistakable relationship between language proficiency and literacy and academic growth. To deny, indeed to not even think, that deaf and hard of hearing students might have similar, if not greater, needs for such programs and language opportunities is a basic denial of equal protection.

NOTES

1. Melanie Gurley Keeney and Stephanie Tueth, "Legal Issues Involving Educating Children with Limited English Proficiency," National School Boards Association, http://www.nsba.org/site/doc_cosa.asp?TRACKID=&CID=164&DID=11273.
2. 35 Fed. Reg. 11,595, as quoted in *Serna v. Portales Municipal Schools*, 499 F.2d 1147, 1153 (10th Cir. 1974).
3. *Lau v. Nichols*, 414 U.S. 563, 569 (1974).
4. *Id.* at 566.
5. *Id.* at 568.
6. 20 U.S.C. § 1703(f).
7. No Child Left Behind Act of 2001, Pub. L. No. 107–110, 115 Stat. 1425, 1690, 1700–1701, 1707 (codified in scattered sections of 20 U.S.C.).

8. U.S. Department of Education, "Declaration of Rights for Parents of English Language Learners," http://www.ed.gov/news/newsletters/extracredit/2004/04/0408.html.

9. Christina M. Rodriguez, "Accommodating Linguistic Difference: Toward a Comprehensive Theory of Language Rights in the United States," *Harvard Civil Rights–Civil Liberties Law Review* 36 (2001): 163, 166.

10. *Castaneda v. Pickard,* 648 F.2d 989, 993 (5th Cir. 1981).

11. *Id.* at 1011.

12. *Id.* at 1013.

13. *Serna v. Portales Municipal Schools,* 499 F.2d 1147 (10th Cir. 1974).

14. *Id.* at 1150.

15. *Id.* at 1154.

16. *Cintron v. Brentwood Union Free School District,* 455 F. Supp. 57, 59 (E.D.N.Y. 1978).

17. *Id.* at 61.

18. *Id.* at 64.

19. *Guadalupe v. Tempe Elementary School District,* 587 F.2d 1022, 1024 (9th Cir. 1978).

20. *Id.* at 1025 n.1.

21. *Id.*

22. 20 U.S.C. § 1703(f).

23. *Hernandez v. New York,* 500 U.S. 352, 371 (1991).

24. *Martin Luther King Jr. Elementary School Children v. Ann Arbor School District,* 473 F. Supp. 1371, 1373 (E.D. Mich. 1979).

25. *Id.* at 1378.

26. *Id.* at 1372.

27. *Id.* at 1381 (emphasis added).

PART 3: CONCLUSIONS AND RECOMMENDATIONS

11

A PROPOSAL

Suit the action to the word, the word to the action.
—William Shakespeare, *Hamlet*

SO WHAT IS to be done here? If in fact our school systems or Congress will not address these matters, then deaf and hard of hearing children, like others before them, should seek remedies in our court system. It is my contention that the time has come to litigate cases for deaf and hard of hearing children based on their First and Fourteenth Amendment rights. Ironically enough, the IDEA in 1975 was the direct result of class-action litigation—*Pennsylvania Association for Retarded Children v. Commonwealth* and *Mills v. Board of Education.*[1]

Some may argue that we should be careful in relying on the First and Fourteenth Amendments. But, as Abraham Lincoln said, "As our case is new, so we must think anew and act anew."[2] And so let the argument for a constitutional right to communication and language stand on its own merits.

Some may ask, and many eventually will, what of the cost, of the institutional impact, should a deaf or hard of hearing child or even an adult assert a constitutional right to communication and language? Will such a child have an absolute right to a qualified interpreter? An absolute right to attend a distant state or center school? An absolute right to require a school to make classrooms acoustically appropriate? Will such a child have the absolute right, based on the Constitution, to be provided communication instruction to ensure the development of age-appropriate language skills?

The answer to all these questions is yes, because the denial of the right is greater than the cost of serving it. I raise here a consti-

147

tutional, not a fiscal or political, question. We have always found ways to serve those needs that are both costly and important. Our values have, at least most of the time, driven our use of resources, and that is as it should be. Consider that the federal government distributes over $1 billion annually for bilingual education.[3] Consider, by way of comparison, the significant cost of making all buildings and public transportation accessible to people in wheelchairs. Prior to the litigation and legislation that led to the requirement of this kind of access, many asked if the cost was really worth the benefit. How do we as a society evaluate these kinds of cost-benefit matters? Ask the individual who can live a more complete life because of those ramps or mechanisms. By focusing primarily on cost, we stop the analysis before it begins.

A LEGISLATIVE PROPOSAL

Congress can and should (and as a result of litigation may be required to) consider federal legislation to address the fundamental questions posed here, in order to ensure that all educational programs serving deaf and hard of hearing children include

1. clear rules, procedures, and programs to provide deaf and hard of hearing children with full and appropriate communication and language *access*, *development*, and *assessment*;
2. teachers and staff who have the skills and training necessary to effectively teach these children and who are proficient in the children's communication mode and language, or certified and proficient interpreters; and
3. a seamless system that brings together the educational, medical, and other related fields so that families with deaf and hard of hearing children have information and services to ensure that children develop communication and language skills at the earliest possible time.

The following proposed legislation represents the thinking of educators, community leaders, parents, and deaf and hard of hearing individuals throughout the nation. It is an amalgam of recommendations made by the U.S. Commission on Education of the Deaf, the National Deaf Education Project, and the National Agenda, a partnership of national family, advocacy, and educational organizations.[4]

The Right to Language and Education Act

The Right to Language and Education Act
A. recognizes that the "starting point" for any educational system for deaf and hard of hearing students (indeed all students) must be that language and communication access and development drive the system; and
B. creates a clear and forceful right of deaf and hard of hearing children to
   1. have unfettered access to rich and varied language environments,
   2. have unfettered access to programs in which there is a critical mass of age, cognitive, and language peers (whether that means peers who are hard of hearing or profoundly deaf),
   3. have unfettered access to programs in which teachers and staff can communicate directly and proficiently with them, and
   4. participate in programs that systemically and successfully provide them the chance to develop age-appropriate language skills in both their native language and English.

Congress finds the following:
A. There are in this nation as many as 1,053,000 individuals under the age of 18 with a reported hearing loss; anywhere from 60,000 to 80,000 children with

a hearing loss were served in special education programs.

B. A hearing loss involves the most basic of human needs, the ability to communicate with other human beings. Many deaf and hard of hearing children use, as their primary communication mode, American Sign Language, whereas others express and receive language through English-based sign systems, or orally and aurally, with or without visual signs or cues.

C. The importance of developing early and effective language and communication skills is fundamental to the educational growth of all children; deaf and hard of hearing children are often denied early opportunities to develop communication skills and as a result enter school with minimal communication skills.

D. Deaf and hard of hearing children, on average, graduate, if at all, from high school with substandard reading and other academic skills, have high rates of illiteracy, and have low rates of college attendance. Deaf and hard of hearing adults have significantly higher rates of unemployment and underemployment and a higher reliance on various forms of governmental assistance.

E. In 1988, the Commission on Education of the Deaf (COED) reported to the Congress and the president of the United States that the status of education for deaf children was unacceptable and recommended fundamental changes in how educational services are delivered to deaf and hard of hearing children, including changes in the way the Individuals with Disabilities Education Act (IDEA) is applied to these children. The National Association of State Directors of Special Education, in its 1994 "Educational Guidelines for Deaf and Hard of hearing Children," reported that because of the unique communication and cultural needs of deaf and hard of hearing children, significant changes in the educational delivery system should be made.

F. Existing law, particularly the IDEA, provides significant assistance to deaf and hard of hearing children and, as reauthorized in 1997, requires that the individualized education program (IEP) team consider a deaf or hard of hearing child's unique communication needs. The IDEA, however, because of its focus on the "least restrictive environment" (LRE), is particularly limiting, as written, for many deaf and hard of hearing children.

G. Congress therefore recognizes that the IDEA should and can be made compatible with the unique needs of deaf and hard of hearing children, and by this Act assures that all deaf and hard of hearing children are provided a quality education in which the educational delivery system for deaf and hard of hearing children is communication and language driven to ensure that programs and services provided for those children address their unique communication needs.

H. A communication- and language-driven educational delivery system will ensure that communication assessment, development, and access and the various programmatic and other components described herein are fundamental to any educational delivery system for deaf and hard of hearing children.

I. In a communication- and language-driven system, all programmatic and fiscal determinations will be based on the unique communication needs of deaf and hard of hearing children.

(a) This Act is designed to be fully compatible with the IDEA, and in addition establishes standards and rules and procedures for educating children who are deaf and hard of hearing, such standards and rules to be specifically incorporated into the IDEA, with all determinations made by an IEP team or any other educational unit to be fully consistent with the requirements described herein.

(b) A child's individual communication and educational needs dictate all components of his or her educational program; this Act does not establish the requirement that one particular educational style or program or one particular communication mode or language be preferred over another, but rather that the child's individual communication needs will determine individual placement and the provision of various services. Deaf and hard of hearing children communicate in very different ways; what constitutes communication assessment, development, and access for an oral child will be very different for a child who uses sign language. Each communication mode and language or system will be recognized, respected, and provided for.

(c) The least restrictive environment under the IDEA for a deaf or hard of hearing child is specifically defined as that classroom and program that provides for the child's communication development and access as described in (d) below and therefore may be a regular classroom, a special classroom or school, or residential placement. By this Act, the right to be educated in a regular classroom is not altered.

To the maximum extent appropriate, children with disabilities who need alternative educational settings have an equal right to such settings. The burden to remove children from a regular educational environment or from an alternative environment rests on the local educational agency, which must demonstrate clear and convincing reasons that the child should be so removed.

(d) Given the importance of a deaf and hard of hearing child's communication needs, the IEP team shall be formally designated as the "IEP/Communication Development Team" for those children. The IEP will include an attached communication and language plan that will provide detail as to how the child will be provided full and appropriate communication and language access and development.

(e) A deaf and hard of hearing child is entitled to an education that provides:

(1) appropriate, early, and ongoing communication and language assessment;

(2) formal, early, and ongoing communication and language development, which includes specific educational programs and services to ensure that the child has age-appropriate communication and language (expressive and receptive) and other academic skills; and

(3) appropriate, early, and ongoing communication and language access, including a critical mass of age and language peers, staff proficient in the child's communication mode, and direct and appropriate communication access to all school activities.

(f) The local and state educational agencies will

(1) recognize and accommodate the individual child's particular hearing loss and unique cultural and linguistic needs;

(2) provide appropriate programs, including all options on the "continuum of placement options" under the IDEA, as well as regional

centers, center schools, and other placement options that can provide for the critical mass, language access, and development necessary for many deaf and hard of hearing children as required by 20 U.S.C. § 1413(h);

(3) provide programs and program components that are communication and language accessible, with professional staff who are appropriately trained, who are fully proficient in the child's individual communication mode and language, and who understand the unique needs of deaf and hard of hearing students;

(4) ensure the development of age-appropriate English writing and reading skills in deaf and hard of hearing students;

(5) develop appropriate curricula, materials, and assessment instruments and implement "best practices";

(6) recognize American Sign Language as a distinct language of deaf people, develop standards for teaching it as a language, and adopt American Sign Language as a foreign language in high school graduation requirements;

(7) recognize and provide for the unique needs of deaf and hard of hearing children who are oral-aural and require an educational environment and program that meets those needs, including, but not limited to, a critical mass of oral-aural peers, appropriately trained staff, and such support services as required to provide for the development of the child's receptive and expressive speech skills, as well as the right of such a child to be in regular education under the IDEA;

(8) develop standards for teachers, sign language

and oral interpreters, and other aides and professionals who work with deaf and hard of hearing students;

(9) develop the highest academic standards for deaf and hard of hearing children and provide services and programs to ensure that they are provided a quality and rigorous educational experience;

(10) develop programs and procedures to ensure that the responsible educational units, including state and local agencies, develop interagency agreements with appropriate health and other institutions and agencies in the various states regarding universal, early identification of hearing loss and effective interface between medical and educational services; and

(11) provide parent and guardian training, referrals to appropriate medical, educational, and community resources, and assistance in developing family language skills.[5]

A FINAL WORD (OR TWO)

Passage of this proposed legislation would help make the following story more likely to be an everyday occurrence:

The child walked into her classroom along with three of her friends. They signed rapidly and easily. They giggled. Tomorrow was her birthday and ten classmates were coming to her house for a party. The teacher waited for the children to sit down and then began to explain the day's work. The teacher signed easily and at an adult level. At 9:30 a.m., the child and two of her classmates left the classroom to meet with the their language specialist in a small room off the library. They worked together for an hour on ASL. The child was eight, but her language skills were at about the level of a five-year-old. The language specialist was confident, however, that she would soon have age-appropriate skills and would then be able to read at her age level as well.

This vignette has a hundred variations, whether the child is able to easily transfer to a state school for the deaf, is oral-aural and is flourishing in an acoustically appropriate school with the necessary aids and services to grow academically and establish meaningful relationships with his hearing peers, is a student with a cochlear implant and is learning to adjust to sound in her classroom, or is a sophomore in high school who, with the aid of a qualified ASL interpreter, is doing well in trigonometry and advanced English. This vignette will, if we have the determination, multiply a thousand times so that a deaf or hard of hearing child's parents will no longer have to fight, year after year, for the most basic elements of an education and will not have to justify their child's right to have language in school.

The *Brown* case marked a profound moment in our history. It meant the beginning of the end of a sordid story. In 1880, a group of hearing educators met in Milan, Italy, and issued a declaration that called for the elimination of manual language in the education of deaf children. It marked the beginning of the end of a way of communicating that was central to the life, culture, and indeed existence of many deaf people. The consequences of that conference were felt well into the twentieth and early twenty-first centuries, and deaf and hard of hearing people have been marginalized and rendered second-class citizens by the policies, beliefs, and decisions of the majority culture for a long time.

In 1938, sixteen years before Thurgood Marshall argued *Brown* before the U.S. Supreme Court, he assisted a sixty-five-year-old African American man who had gone to the Dallas, Texas, courthouse to take his seat as a juror. The man was told by officials that he ought to excuse himself, but when the junior-college president refused, he was grabbed, taken outside, and thrown down the front steps of the courthouse.[6] In September 1957, nine African American students walked with the same dignity as the Texas juror, but with a phalanx of federal troops, into Central High School in Little Rock, Arkansas, to assume their full rights as American citizens.

Approximately twenty years later, Amy Rowley walked into her kindergarten class in New York State. There were no troops; there was no hateful mob trying to stop her. But she too was denied her full and rightful place. She too was viewed as somehow not quite like all the other students and therefore not in need of the full range of educational experiences that the rest of her class took for granted. She too was denied very fundamental rights—in this case, the right to know what other students and her teachers were discussing.

Deaf and hard of hearing students, like all other students, deserve the chance to learn and use language, to become literate, to be proud of who they are, and to engage in life. This is what our Constitution protects. This is why the Constitution is a living, vital document, but perhaps more importantly, a fundamentally American creation. Amy Rowley and all her deaf and hard of hearing peers are entitled to repose under that Constitution—like the plaintiffs in *Brown;* like the children in Little Rock, like all our children.

NOTES

1. *Pennsylvania Association for Retarded Children v. Commonwealth,* 334 F. Supp. 1257 (E.D. Pa. 1971); *Mills v. Board of Education,* 348 F. Supp. 866 (D.D.C. 1972).

2. Roy P. Basler, *Abraham Lincoln: His Speeches and Writings* (Cleveland, Ohio: World Publishing, 1946), 668.

3. U.S. Department of Education, Office of English Language Acquisition, home page, http://www.ed.gov/offices/OELA (accessed August 28, 2007).

4. Commission on Education of the Deaf, *Toward Equality: Education of the Deaf; A Report to the President and Congress of the United States* (Washington, D.C.: Government Printing Office, 1988); Lawrence Siegel, *Educational and Communication Needs of Deaf and Hard of Hearing Children: A Statement of Principle Regarding Fundamental Systemic Educational Changes*

(Greenbrae, Calif.: National Deaf Education Project, 2000); *The National Agenda: Moving Forward on Achieving Educational Equality for Deaf and Hard of Hearing Students* (Austin, Texas: Texas School for the Deaf, 2005).

5. *Veazey v. Ascension Parish School Board,* 40 I.D.E.L.R. (LRP) 179, at 737–739 (M.D. La. 2004).

6. Richard Kluger, *Simple Justice* (New York: Vintage Books, 1975), 222–223.

INDEX

79; right to annoy and, 82–83; right
to be with peers and, 68–70; Rowley
case and, 7
Flynt, Larry, 90
Fourteenth Amendment: equal protection of
law and, 95–97; excerpt from, 93;
Plyler v. Doe and, 111–13; rights recognized under, xiii, xiv, 11; right to
education under, 101–3, 113–14;
Rowley case and, 7; *Serrano v. Priest*
and, 108–11; tests of equal protection, 97–101
free and appropriate public education
(FAPE), 55
freedom to communicate, 49–52

Gallaudet University, 126
gender-based test of equal protection, 100
governmental assistance, reliance on, 31
*Guadalupe v. Tempe Elementary School Dis-
trict*, 138–39

Hague Recommendations on Education
Rights of National Minorities, 19
Hand, Learned, 86
hateful communication, 85–86
hearing children, communications between
deaf children and, 36–37
hearing parents, experience of, 12
Herodotus, 49–50
Hirabayashi v. United States, 99
Holmes, Oliver Wendell, 51
human dignity and language, 19–20
human experience, communication and language and, 17–18
Hustler magazine, 90

IDEA. *See* Individuals with Disabilities Education Act (IDEA)
ideas, exchange of, 81–82
IEP, communication needs in, 7, 56
illegal immigrants, education for, 111–13
illiteracy, Supreme Court on, 112
immutable characteristics, 99

income, average, 31
Individuals with Disabilities Education Act
(IDEA): conflicts with, xiv; courts
and, 58–61; devaluation of communication and language under, 47, 82;
dispute resolution process, 57; due
process hearings, 5, 64–67, 78; equal
protection of law and, 96–97; failings under, 4, 10; First Amendment
and, 54–58; integrationist nature of,
135–36; least restrictive environment
(LRE) provision of, 4–5, 8, 55–56,
63–64; mainstreaming and, 33; reau-
thorization of, 7; related services, 7,
38, 54–55; requirements under, 4; re-
visions to, 10–11
information, free flow of: commercial information, 86–89; dangerous speech
and, 80; denial of, 82; education
and, 102; First Amendment and,
47–49; hateful communication and,
85; in schools, 52–54
integration, 135–36
international law and language, 19–20
interpreted education, 37–40
isolation of deaf and hard of hearing children: least restrictive environment
and, 4–5, 8, 55–56, 63–64; mainstreaming and, 34, 69; Rowley and,
xii–xiii; vignette example, 14–17

Jefferson, Thomas, 12
Jehovah's Witnesses, 82–83

Keating, Elizabeth, 36–37
Keller, Helen, 35

Lamont v. Postmaster General, 52
language: culture and, 118, 119, 121–22,
133; definition of, 18; human dignity
and, 19–20; importance of, and right
to, 117–23; international law and,
19–20. *See also* communication and
language; development of language

CPSIA information can be obtained
at www.ICGtesting.com
Printed in the USA
FFOW05n1205080115